A House Divided

By C. J. Henning

Createspace

Copyright 2018

Other works published by C. J. Henning available at Amazon.com, Barnes and Noble, Booksamillion, Trillion Books and other outlets. Some available on Kindle.

Fantasy

The Saga of Everstream-Tiathan Eiula and the War of the Seven Fortresses, Vol. 1 & 2.
Whirlwind Sage and the Arbushi Wars

Nursery Rhyme and Fairy Tale Mysteries
More Mysteries of Fairy Tales and Nursery Rhymes

Drama

The Plays Vol. 1 & 2

Commentaries

Common Sense or Who's That Sitting In My Pew?
Common Sense, Too or Are You Still Sitting In My Pew?
I Will Not Apologize For Christ
Death And Dying, A Cautionary Uplifting Commentary

Fiction

Wormwood

On the Morning of The First Day
The Last Messiah

Children's Books

Tittle Tattle Tales
John Taddlebock and The Weegie Worts
A Walk In The Dark
Monsters And Ghosts
I Thought I Saw...

Poetry

Complete Poetry 1968-2000
Patriot Dreams and Dreams of God
Cathedral
Nonsense Rhymes
More Nonsense Rhymes
Even More Nonsense Rhymes
Risen And Rising
Random Thoughts Of An Old Man
Thinking Of Love
Love Abounds
Whispering Sweet Nothings
Death and Other Party Favor
Visions of Love

"If a house is divided against itself,
that house cannot stand."

        Mark 3:25

"Do you bring in a lamp to put under a bowl or a bed? Instead why don't you put it on a stand? For whatever is concealed is meant to be disclosed, and whatever is concealed is meant to brought out into the open. If anyone has ears to hear, let him hear."

        Mark 4: 21-23

"Then the King will say to those on his right 'Come you who are blessed by my father; take your inheritance, the kingdom prepared for you since the creation of the world. For I was hungry and you gave me something to eat. I was a stranger and you invited me in. I needed clothes and you clothed me. I was sick and you looked after me. I was in prison and you came to visit me.'

Then the righteous will answer him, 'Lord when did we see you hungry and fed you, or thirsty and gave you something to drink? When did we see you a stranger and invite you in or needed clothes and clothed you? When did we see you sick or in prison and go to visit you?'

The King will reply: 'I tell you the truth. Whatever you did for one of the least of these brothers of mine, you did for me.'"

        Matthew 25: 24-40

Introduction

I thought hard before writing this ponderous tome of self-inflicted wounds called a personal history of my life. You'll excuse my apologies for looking at the reasons the Lord watched over me for so many years. Mediocrity and confusion, murder and mayhem, illness and near death were just a part of the road I took.

God decided that a game of chess was in order to keep me safe from the cruelty of my family growing up and the abuse found at school. My mother, the Queen, held sway knocking us kids around as mere pawns without excusing the gambit of emotions. Eventually it led to murder and destruction of family ties. Welcome to the madness and mayhem with a flicker of light from the Lord.

What is there to believe in if there is nothing to believe in? If God exists, would God allow such terrible things to happen in life? How often can someone delve into the psychology of murder? What brought the killer to the point of desperation to act? How long before the event? Could it have been prevented? Was it premeditated, a crime of passion or temporary madness?

This true story involves how my brother and I had the same upbringing, but it led him to life imprisonment while I was left without family for not giving up on him and just general misunderstanding from gossip.

Paul, my brother, and I are invisible in our own way. Paul disappeared within the house that was his prison and now prison is his house. I still will not forsake him and for that the Lord has come into his life.

We are all fallible of creatures even when we accept the Lord. The difference between those that believe and those that don't is the resurrection of Christ Jesus. We still sin but are more conscious of the sin. We berate ourselves and try again. Though we believe, we doubt. Though we are saved, we doubt. Though we know God exists, we doubt. We are only human.

One last thought about being a Christian is the following:

> To the powerful we are just dust,
> To the rich we are pennies left on the ground,
> Yet to God we are clouds that float above
> Until the sun evaporates the years of life
> To rain upon, with our joy of Christ,
> On those who see only shadows and despair.
>
>   Complete Poetry - Henning

Chapter One
Almost a Non-beginning

Everyone has had a sad tale to tell so why should this one be any different concerning the tragedy that unfolded on the Thanksgiving weekend of 2004. How does a home become a "Horror House" with passersby looking into the basement windows to see blood or, at least, a ghost or two wandering the dark corners? How terrible could it have been that a son would kill his mother and older brother whom he lived with?

To start I should not be here to write this book. It is a miracle in itself that I have survived so long while others who were healthier passed by the wayside. The Lord decided that He had other plans and hopefully it includes finishing this before He calls me home.

Looking back, I believe the Lord had His hand on my shoulder and never let go. It was years later before I fully acknowledged He was there. If He wasn't, only disaster would have followed. I felt His presence, but I went my own way till He put up roadblocks to go His way.

Everything makes sense when a missing piece of a puzzle presents itself. On a November night in 1977, my father and I were walking to the movies since neither of us had a car or a driver's license. He suddenly turned to me to say "You know...Your mother and I were thinking of aborting you." That's all he said. I was dumbfounded, but if I could have thought faster I might have said "Thanks for sharing, Dad." Or maybe "If you did, you wouldn't be going to the movies because I'm paying." What father would say this to his son and tell him that he wished I was never born? Abortion negates birth.

It did explain the aloofness of my father. He never held us or comforted us. There were times he brought me along for events, but we never talked about anything important.

A year later I was told that my father wanted to leave my mother, but having two children and Catholic, albeit one who was excommunicated, made it impossible. My father blamed me for his unhappy life. It could not have been too miserable since three more children were produced. My mother said a few times that she wished she had all girls instead of four boys and a girl. Another inkling why we were treated the way we were.

    My father lost his father early in life when he stepped on a rusty nail and died from an infection. His stepfather was a police chief, but he wasn't the most affectionate of men. I remember him sitting in chair with his back to me holding a glass of beer and smoking a cigar. One day he asked if I wanted a swig of his German green beer. I must have been nine or ten years old at the time and thought that he seemed to enjoy the drink. It made me sick instead and was a leading cause why I do not drink to this day. The same happened with the cigar. One hapless day he gave me his cigar and said "Take a deep suck on this." I did and was coughing and throwing up. He thought it was funny, but it helped to keep me from smoking as well.

    My dad was more of an absent father who sometimes took me to ball games. There was never any sage advice for any of us. He was disappointed with everyone and needed to stay away from home by working six days a week. Part of that was to get overtime to pay the bills.

    Having to be unwanted at birth gave me a sense that

the Lord has been with me all my life. I just didn't understand or try to notice He was walking with me all the time. I came into the world unwanted except for what the Lord had in store for me. More of a life of Job than the apostle Paul. No thorn in my side except to jump into the whole bush and come out a spiritual porcupine.

Where does one get lost in the journey that you thought was a straight road? So many side streets prey on the soul leading to a forgetfulness of the purpose of the journey. What lay down these side streets were sex, power, evil intent, good intentions, bad judgment, mediocre decisions, cowardice, sexual deviation, attempted suicide and unlimited siren calls to pull our family apart.

The siren's call because their journey had ended and the only entertainment they had was pulling others to their own destruction. This is a true story of a family lost through the eyes of myself and my brother Paul because the siren calls were so great that we could only be found in a corner shivering from our own guilt. It is, also, a story of redemption and the saving grace of Jesus the Christ.

Why is it that as you pray, you dream of adultery? As you pray, you show anger against others? As you pray, you yearn to win the lottery? As you pray, you become deaf to God's voice? As you pray, you only speak of you? This is what God hears and that was the life that was ahead of me until later when I understood that the Lord was the focus and the things I prayed for were dust.

I learned through a rough life, which I will get to, that God said I should learn first if I am your God or you will only hear yourself. God said I am not a horn of plenty spilling out riches and success for a fee of tithes and offerings. God said I do not accept grocery lists of convenience though sincere confession is good for the soul and it is not a down payment to continue sinning.

God, also, helped me understand that He is here as my God so that I will, not should, follow Him, obey Him and worship Him. He blesses as He sees fit not as I demand. God tells us that He is the Alpha and Omega as we are only the iota in the alphabet of life. Without God, we are worthless to ourselves and those around us. Without God, we are finite dust. Without God we waste our breath with only meaningless words and empty greatness.

God continues to tell us that without Him there is no church, no chance of peace, no hope of resurrection through Christ and no reason to strive for the good of mankind. If the Lord took His hand from the world it would be no more. Not because He wills, but because we do. God does not say this to be cruel, but He knows the minds of men.

Being unwanted at birth strangely made it easier to accept the little contact I have with other family members through indifference, gossip, rumors and anger that has lasted over 45 years. I have not suffered greatly being estranged from my family as it affected my brother Paul being so close around it.

The damage done during my childhood still hides in the dark corners of my mind and leap out in the middle of the night at times. Being estranged has healed me because of distance and disassociation. I had been judged and deemed unworthy by my family. My sentence was to be banned, exiled from them forever.

My wife and children were never to be acknowledged for recognition was a sign of weakness on their part. Foolishly or not, if I was called, I would answer. I do not have the bitterness but do have the caution.

Now the reader is thinking this is going to be a dreary book about a woe is me life. Woe is Cliffie. Suck it up then. I have lived with tragedy, hate and violence for the first part of my life and I praise the Lord for it! Why? Was it my goal to be a backlashing monk? No, the Lord gave me insight and the gift of discernment that I pushed from the darkness into the light through my life's adventure.

It is easy to list problems, accomplishments, self-pity, love and hate in a life's story. However, how do you show God's love, patience and intervention? What makes a testimony if you tiptoe between humbleness and pride? It is hard not to sound boastful or pitiful when recounting hardships, failures and difficulties of your life that have been overcome with faith. Not all is forgotten and age has a knack of rewarding a long life with reminders of failures and successes whether you want to remember them or not.

Again, I say, suck it up and continue reading of a man who grew up in a hateful and angry family that didn't realize how much they needed Christ. Unfortunately, I didn't know how my faith could help them. This is not a whiney baby testimony or a feel sorry for me story for I have overcome with the Lord's help and His blessing to live this long.

I spent most of my life away from my family, but I put the Cross and the burden of their suffering on myself. As a Christian why could I not change anything? I realized nothing was the answer. Each of us had our hidden terrors and nightmares we had to deal with. Ghosts of the past wait in the corners when my faith staggers because I wished the Lord could have saved my family as well.

I yearned for what could never be. I savor what I have with my wife and children. I just hope I did not bring any of this evil that is left into their lives. Sometimes I feel like I have a thorn in my side, a spear, a noose around my neck with an Albatross on my head. Yet, the Lord my God loves me still. You might ask how I can be assured of His love? Because I am still living on borrowed time (67 years and counting) I am now retired with a loving family and memorable unique experiences that counteract the sad memories.

I spoke of borrowed time because as I stated earlier, my parents thought about aborting me. Moving forward in time, I believe I was nine years old when I went into convulsions and was taken to the hospital. Before I was taken, I had to be put into a tub of ice for the fever was so high. I had an advanced form of Tonsillitis. At the hospital, the doctors took out my tonsils.

As I was recovering, I contracted Rheumatic Fever which put me in a coma. I woke up momentarily with probes on my head attached to a monitor. I looked over to see the doctor talking to my parents and he said "You need to prepare yourself. Your son has a pinhole in his heart. If it doesn't heal...He may be living on borrowed time..."

I drifted off again. My heart was scarred for life and the doctor wasn't giving me a great chance to survive. While in the hospital it was decided later that I had to have a dose of Mumps and Chicken Pox before I could go home. I was told for the next couple of years no contact sports, no excitement or agitation. So, I went to school, but came home sitting in a chair or couch watching T.V. I have to say whatever show was on T.V., I saw it.

A small event which I'll add to show how our efforts to amuse ourselves brought the wrong outcome. At the age of thirteen, I discovered the wonderful world of plastic guns that shot little flying discs. My brother Paul and I spent an afternoon in our bedroom shooting a thousand of those little suckers until our mother came up complaining about the noise we were making. She chased us downstairs then came back, vacuumed all of the discs and threw away the guns.

At the age of 14, I decided I had had enough of being

by myself and not playing with the other kids. I was told not to play contact sports, but as I walked home from school, my classmates were playing tackle football. Being young and stupid, I asked to play. On the third play, Bill Bushel, a big kid, plowed into me. I remember being nearby a group of kids looking down at someone. I heard someone ask "Is he dead?" I could hear and see and wanted to know who it was and I seemed to float above them. Just as I was going to see who it was I woke up lying on the ground. I still believe it was an out of body experience.

That experience later, looking back, proved there is a spirit inside us that when we die leaves the body behind. It proved to me that there is an afterlife and we can expect a reckoning.

I waited until I was 15 and cleared to exercise again by my doctor. I then started up in track and field and baseball. It ended up being difficult to play any sport because I suffered with boils from 1964-1968. Contact sports were impossible. The boils on my face, back and chest were incredibly bad. My brothers had mild cases of acne, but I got the scourge. I felt like the Frankenstein monster and my classmates were the local peasants that wanted to drive me from their sight.

I withdrew into myself by drawing and long lonely walks. I involved myself within the church and school by singing in the choir and attaching my art with Mr. Dawson, an art teacher. I had a lot of imagination to overcome the trials of my family and schoolmates.

My singing in High School helped me to join a local Up With People! Group. I was a soloist that sang "What Color Is God's Skin?" We toured Westchester County with a group of thirty or more teenagers. I could hide behind the singing and it took me away from some of my shyness.

Singing was a way to show a talent where I had no ear for playing an instrument. Being a teenager without friends, I had to find whatever talents I could use to get attention. The same was for the artwork and art shows that heaped praise on my ego.

Chapter Two

House of Horrors

Sadly, house of horrors was the name given to our family home. It wasn't bad enough our family was isolated in our community, but our background was so varied that few people knew how to approach us. In 1990, my brother Paul said he found a link to our family with Jewish heritage concerning the Mahler's who were my Godparents. Our great grandfather was said to be Jewish.

It was then I realized an opportunity to be unique among my Christian brethren. My father was Catholic, albeit ex-communicated and my mother insisted we go to the Presbyterian Church. So, when I was asked my faith, I would say I was a Jewlicaterian. Jewish, Catholic, Presbyterian with a tag line that if someone mentioned a joke about a minister, a priest and a rabbi going into a bar, I would say I was offended no matter who went in first.

It didn't go over well most of the time, but I felt twice blessed having a Jewish heritage and a Christian one. Who can say differently?

Growing up though, my mother was a tyrant and how my parents stayed together was a sad miracle in itself. Having tormented my father and knowing I was the cause of his misery, my mother would make sure I had extra gifts on birthdays and Christmas. It, also, isolated me from my brothers and sister.

I am getting ahead of myself and the events leading up to that fateful day of family disintegration. To understand the depth of anger and psychological perversion of our lives we must understand where it came from.

I was told by my mother that my father seldom held us. We were bottle fed because my mother drank too much. She had a distance from us boys because "she wished she had all girls." It explained many things.

Throughout my childhood, my parents would fight and argue while my mother would turn to me and ask with a fierce look: "Who's right? Me or your father?" If my answer was "Dad." There would be hell to pay for the next couple of days. Cries of "How could you take his side?" or "You don't love me!" are still faint echoes in my mind.

Another loving feature of favorite sayings from my mother was "If you don't like it here, leave!" and she held open the back door. The terrifying thing was that I believed she meant it. One less mouth to feed. My sister said she heard her say it before, but I never knew that until she told me later in life.

After my stint in the hospital, I was laid up watching T.V. shows which encouraged me to be an artist, I wanted to do something besides sit. I used watercolor and enamel paint to do artwork of clowns and flowers to escape the soap opera of my family.

I spent hours walking up and down streets with a red wagon to collect bottles whereby I could get two cents from deposits listed on the bottles. Unfortunately, I used the money to buy candy and soda which eventually after long abuse set off my diabetes.

I entered art shows and was able to sell some of my work. I painted images on t-shirts, which at an art show by my church, three businessmen walked in and bought all ten of my shirts. I convinced myself later that I started the t-shirt craze, but not smart enough to market them. My family was not impressed.

Something that relates to my artwork was when I was 19 and worked at Playland Amusement Park renting row boats and electric boats on the lake. Mr. Tolve, my boss, heard about my work and saw me painting a small speedboat I purchased. He asked if I would paint some images for the channel that his paddle boat ride passed through with customers.

I used 4x8 plywood boards making tigers, lions and other animals. I worked three summers there and made an unusual friend who showed how naïve I was with life in general. Moving ahead for now, I'll try not to go through time, but my past tends to be disjointed in fractured memories.

His name was Rich who seemed to be a local drug dealer as well. Even when he invited me to a party at his friend's house, I was oblivious to it all. We first went to a broken-down house and I went with Rich upstairs. As he was talking and dealing I was looking out the window. The two guys demanded "What are you looking for?" Thinking I might be a narc they hurried us outside.

Now I am sitting on a couch at this house watching the activities around me, still not understanding what kind of party it was that I had gone to. I was still waiting for the cake and soda. I did think it strange that so many were smoking something strange and popping pills.

I never once thought the police might break in. One bearded guy stood and stared at a light bulb. It was then the only girl in the room, who served pills on a plate, came over and said "You don't belong here. You should go home." So, I did.

At Playland Lake, my second year working there, a gang of youths from New York City took over three rides sending them at maximum speed for twenty minutes before the police came. They escaped to where we were, but we had already pushed out the wooden and aluminum boats before we jumped in aluminum boats ourselves. I was the closest when I saw them looking down from the arcade. They used zip guns and shot three times my way. The bullets hit the side of my boat while I lay flat. The police came before any of us were hurt.

Amusing things happened that come to mind. One was a time I was patrolling the lake making sure everyone was safe. The boats were hourly rentals so we took turns keeping tab. This particular afternoon, I spied two women who were sunbathing nude and a separate boat with a man sunbathing nude. I greeted the young ladies as I passed by and took in the guy with his boat. He demanded why I didn't bring the girls in. I replied "What girls?"

The second event that sticks in my mind was a fact that each boat had a weight limit of 900 lbs. However, these four 300+ gentlemen insisted on renting only one boat. I told them there was too much weight, but they laughed at me. I held the boat for them as they got in. There was maybe two inches between the top of the boat and the water. I gently pushed them from the dock. At the first stroke of an oar, the boat sank. They were waste deep in water and cried out for help. I said "But you still have 59 minutes left on your rental."

I got involved with my church under the protection of Rev. Theobald, Mrs. Castelli, the choir director and Mrs. Langham, the church secretary. Those three kept a safety blanket over me so I would not hear those in the church congregation who would have nothing to do with my family.

We never had friends or family over the house. We did go to get-togethers of family each year. My mother was a gossip and instigator which probably had much to do with it. The Lord kept a security blanket on me though I had not made a commitment. The Lord already decided to watch over me and bided His time till I woke up to him.

I need to go back to my childhood where things were setting up my future as an insecure adult. I think the word would be naïve in so many ways which also saved me in other ways.

Growing up alone, though I had three brothers and a sister, I spent many lonely days playing with Civil War figures, cowboys against Indians, World War II soldiers to make great war scenarios involving all of them. I had sets of Lincoln Logs, castles to build forts and lines of defense against overwhelming odds. I learned my own strategies to amuse myself since my brothers and sister had no time for me.

I get teary eyed even now when I watch a movie where brothers and sisters are either close or reconcile in the end. We could not be close because my mother would not allow it. She felt if she could not be loved then no one would enjoy the comfort it would have brought. That part of my life has been lost and the emptiness in that mist of my soul has never filled the loneliness until I met my wife. Even though I accepted Christ, the guilt still wanders in the darker corners of my mind.

When I was recovering from Rheumatic Fever and problems with my heart, I instigated a small squabble with my brothers and sister. As they argued amongst themselves, I took my seat on a lounge chair and watched TV. My mother came in and screamed at them to stop before she said "Why can't you be like Cliff and just quietly watch TV?"

My brother Glenn complained: "But he started it!" My mother shook her head in disbelief. It was then I realized I had a hidden gift. The gift of instigating trouble and not get caught.

There are many things about my childhood I don't remember. I was told I was difficult and I did some cruel things. Two come to mind concerning Kindergarten and Second Grade. The first was a temper tantrum for whatever reason and was told to go to the Principal's office. As I left I kicked down sandcastles that were constructed in the middle of the room. It was a unique experience to have a constructed barrier with sand to keep the children quiet.

I was sent to Mr. Marshall's office. who was a gracious gentleman who knew my family. He was very patient with me as I cried in his arms. He watched over me until fourth or fifth grade when I think he retired. He made excuses so no record would show up in my school files.

The second thing was a story someone told me in high school where a girl said something I didn't like in second grade and I pushed her into a line of bushes as we walked home. I must have been an angry child though so much even now I could not remember.

Those things I remember are selective. In second grade, a classmate was being spanked by our teacher. I hid my face behind a book so I wouldn't add to his embarrassment. The teacher thought I was laughing and decided to spank me as well.

In fourth or fifth grade, I engineered a plan to have everyone in the class make a paper airplane and throw them all at once when the teacher turned to write on the blackboard. She turned back too soon and one hit her right on the nose. We all laughed till we saw the anger in her face. She asked who instigated this? Everyone in the classroom pointed to me. So much for loyalty and taking individual responsibility.

I started to gain weight in sixth grade and unable to

keep up in physical education. When I could not do a sit up or pull up, the coach nicknamed me "Hercules" He didn't realize my heart condition would not allow me to exercise properly. He took great delight in pointing out my frail condition.

In seventh grade, my friend Louis decided he was now my enemy. I never knew what made him turn against me. He had two friends who, with him, would regularly push me around and beat me. My father demanded I never fight back and so I took the abuse.

In eighth grade, the three of them took turns pounding on my back and arms as I stood there unmoving with a big crowd of fellow students watching, but not helping. The four of us were sent to the Assistant Principles' office. My father was called in, but not the other fathers.

The Assistant Principle explained that I started the fight with the other three which I did not. My father looked at him incredulously and said "Three against one! Are you kidding me?" He then asked where the other fathers were but was told since I started the fight it wasn't necessary.

I said: "Dad, I didn't fight back." My father said: "I will teach my son to defend himself then." This surprised the

Assistant Principle. I was impressed because my father showed concern for me in public and possibly a sign of affection. It was rare. Maybe he was just embarrassed that a son of his would not fight back.

In ninth grade, Louis and his friends tried to drown me in the high school pool. I was able to escape and get away. Later that year, Louis tried to break my glasses and I fought him to get them back. The Math teacher came in and immediately took me to the Principles' office. She assumed I started the fight even though I told her what happened.

One thing I realized was that God had wound His way into a family so bent on self-destruction and was protecting me. However, it was not all anger and abuse. We played games on Friday nights like Monopoly, Easy Money and card games. We had a regiment of meals that came from my parent's army life. Fish on Friday, Grilled Cheese on Sunday, Meatloaf on Mondays etc.

Other than those times at dinner or game nights, we did not socialize. If we played too loud it meant the belt. If we did not come to the table fast enough it would mean the belt. I remember times I heard my mother coming up the stairs after she was drinking and grumbling about something so I would hide in the closet. This would anger her more and if she found me, it would mean a beating.

While I am reminiscing, let's go back to fifth grade. I spent much of my time at the Harrison Presbyterian Church. I eventually joined the Chancel and later the Senior Choir. As the years went by, I joined their basketball team and headed their youth group. It kept me away from home.

Also, as a teen I joined DeMolay and worked my way up to Chevalier Knight when I realized being a Mason was not in my future. I cannot speak against DeMolay since I had good friends from the experience. I, also, became a bowling champion in a series of tournaments until I damaged my hand. I had thought of going pro, but the injury made it impossible.

I did have bragging rights since I told my father he needed to join me in the Disney Father-Son tournament. We came in second and I had high series. We came home with three trophies that day.

Later that year I needed to impress this girl I knew, Laura, and asked if she wanted a bowling trophy. Yes, I was that sure of myself. She thought I was a little cocky but agreed. We won the tournament and she told me years later that she still had the trophy on her piano. She was a classy lady. I had a crush on her, but I was not on her level.

How does this fit in with my brother, Paul, and later my realizing that the Lord had always been with me? It is necessary to know the different roads that I could have taken though eventually would have found the same Savior. Unfortunately. Paul had to end up in prison before making his decision.

Paul and I were never close, neither was I close to my younger brother and sister. However, I hung out with my older brother, Glenn, and his friends for a short time. My best friend, Roy, was a year older than I was and I really enjoyed his company, too.

Glenn had two friends called Tiny and Dewey. Tiny was a giant of a man and Dewey with big ears was like a Disney character. We played tag football and basketball. Then everything fell apart. The change was more with my brother Glenn than it was with me.

Chapter Three
All Good Things End

Two events stopped the good times with my brother, Glenn, and his friends. One last good thing was the time Glenn and I were rough housing in our upstairs room. Our mom burst in with her infamous belt and threatened to beat us. My brother took the belt away from her and said: "You'll never beat us again!" I appreciated that he said "us". After that day, our mom didn't beat me or Glenn again, but she did beat Paul, my younger brother.

The two events that happened to change everything involved a parakeet and Glenn starting to drink before moving to live in the basement. The parakeet's name was "Petey" and Glenn spent hours training Petey to rub noses, wake us up in the morning for school by dancing on our foreheads then nibble on our ears. If we did not get up when Petey danced on our heads, he would poop on our nose.

One day I was in my room and Paul was working on something at his desk in which he didn't want to be disturbed. I left but forgot to close the bedroom door. Petey always flew to whoever was going downstairs, land on our heads and then flew back to his cage. It was his way of saying goodbye.

This day, Petey flew back to his cage as Paul slammed the door for seclusion. Petey and the door met at the same time which broke its neck. When Glenn came home he blamed Paul and I for his death. He spent more time after that in the basement making himself a room and used the basement door to go in and out.

The second thing was Glenn's drinking and picking up women at the local bar. At one point he was accused of a sexual attack against one of the women he met. She said she was pregnant, but the baby wasn't his and the case dismissed. It was a traumatic experience and put him in almost a permanent dark place. He wanted nothing to do with the family while he hid deeper in the valley of the bottle.

Years later, while my parents were playing cards with my father's sister and husband, two police officers burst in with guns drawn. My mother immediately declared "We're only playing for pennies!"

What had happened was that Glenn had rushed out of the house through the basement door and in his delirium thought someone was in the house to kill him. He ran down the street in his socks to the nearest telephone booth and called the police. He was brought to a hospital for evaluation.

It was the first of four trips to the hospital to help Glenn dry out. The fourth time was when my father and I went to visit him. The doctor told Glenn his family was there to see him. He said "I have no family." He mentioned his girlfriend was his only family.

My father and I left without a word until the parking lot. My dad finally said "To hell with all of you." He was crying and I realized he included me. It was the second time he expressed his disdain for all of us.

Growing up, my father worked hard. He would work six days a week, but because of his lack of education never got into upper management. We thought, as kids, it was to get away from us, but it was to keep from being berated day after day from our mom besides the bills that were mounting up. He needed the overtime.

I remember old home movie clips where he watched us sledding and dropping shovels full of snow on our heads as we sped by, but soon after that he was seldom seen.

During football season for Harrison High School he was a devoted fan bringing Glenn and I to the games. Sometimes we went to Yankee Stadium and Madison Square Garden. At the Garden we watched Notre Dame play and my father had the team sign a small basketball with all their names. Unfortunately, when I put it on the mantle and didn't try to preserve it, the ball deflated into a mass of plastic goo.

There were good times such as my grandmother Susan Haviland, my father's mother, who lost her first husband from an infection by stepping on a rusty nail. Her second husband was Chief of Police in Harrison who I can only remember his cigars and green beer. I mentioned this earlier, but now am expanding the experience.

My grandmother, my father's mother, was a stitch who taught me how to cheat at cards. She comforted me when it was rough at home which meant I spent a lot of time in her apartment. She could have been a refuge from bullies in Jr.

High School, but she was gone by then.

My father's mother was vastly different from my mother's father and mother. Mae and Harry Strong were not a match made in heaven. Mae was a vicious cruel woman who berated my mother in front of me when I was young. I felt a bond with the movie "The Wizard of Oz" because I had Glenda the Good Witch and the Wicked Witch of the West on both sides of the family.

My evil grandmother, Mae, died when I was around ten of complications from Diabetes. My good grandmother died from an accident. My mother's father, Harry, was a rogue. He had a mistress and was a gambler.

It was a family story that he won and lost the only hotel on the Panama Canal playing cards when he was supposedly working there under Theodore Roosevelt. I found it hard to believe until I came into possession of his medals and gold watch from President Roosevelt.

My father had a life of misery in marriage, business and health. I inherited that legacy in health, but not business or marriage. When he died, true to his life, he gave me nothing, not even a pat on the back. I represented the freedom he had lost since I left New York for South Carolina to escape the madness. There was no reconciliation, no parental love, no guidance and no fatherly advice.

Chapter Four

And Now For Something Completely Different

The biggest event in my life in the teen years of acne and boils, was when I was sent to Christian summer camp. It led to love, self-assurance and a closer step with the Lord.

Now I have to back up to eighth grade where I did not only have acne, but boils on my face, chest and back. I was the Frankenstein monster of my class, of my school. No one else considered me so hideous as I felt about myself. I became bitter and angry because I believed I would never date or find love. I would never marry and be a hermit for the rest of my life.

Then I went to summer camp and met M. M. was beautiful though she thought herself plain. She picked me out of a crowd and spent the week with me which changed my life. She both saved and ruined my life. I was at the crossroads of despair and failure, but God would not have me go down that road.

She was my first love and I was hooked. However, she didn't see it that way which I learned years later. The first year after camp we wrote letters to each other. She sprayed perfume on the letters and signed them "Always, M." I thought I was in heaven until the following year at camp.

She lived 40 miles away and if I could have walked that far, I would have seen her before then. The second year of camp was a disaster since she was now not interested in me. She seemed to pick up stray dogs and made them feel wanted. I was confused and made the best of camp.

I met a redhead who helped the doldrums, but on that Friday the whole camp went to a campfire on the lake. As we were leaving, everyone got lost. The redhead and I decided to venture off the path to find our way out. I ended up stepping on a yellow jacket nest where everyone got stung.

I found out that night I was allergic to bee stings. Add that to acne, boils, rheumatic heart and bad eyesight was only the beginning of life long problems. My night ended in a dark room and a swollen leg listening to the singing in the distance.

I came home depressed and what happens? M. sends me a perfumed letter with the familiar "Always, M." Do I discard it? Of course not! I'm still hooked and write back as if nothing happened.

Now you are wondering how this has anything to do with my testimony. I'm showing the progression of a path that the Lord put me on as He set up roadblocks and one-way signs on the road of life.

Anyway, now I have a fantasy girlfriend. That year I joined "Up With People". A local chapter where I met P. who comes on to me and soon we are a couple. Now I have a real girlfriend as well as a fantasy one. Best of both worlds. P. also drives and is very affectionate. My dreams are of M., but my days are with P.

I still believed I was ugly and the boils were getting worse. I saw doctors who used saline solution to relieve the pressure, but left scars on my chest, back and face. It didn't help any when I used a razor blade to puncture the boils. The scars were permanent and I saw a cruel face when I looked into the mirror. I heard others calling me "Crater face" and "dog face".

The next year, I get a letter from M. that she was going to Nyack Missionary College across the Hudson River. Like a good faithful puppy, I get the idea to go there, too.

Mr. Dawson, my art teacher, who had me enter many art competitions wanted me to go to art school and would have gotten me a full scholarship. I was not thinking with my brain so turned him down. If I did go to art school, my life would have been completely different and I believe the Lord knew this. So much for a brain. Love for someone who did not love me was a powerful bit of stupidity but looking back the best possible outcome was in the future.

Mr. Dawson saw some great talent in me that I did not take seriously. I won an advertising contest in my senior year, entered three art shows and painted t-shirts. I sold everything I did. Yet, for me it was a lark.

I almost reconsidered art school until I got a letter from M. inviting me to hear a certain speaker at Nyack College. My brother. Glenn, drove me to the campus. M. came in late and sat on the other side of the building. I waited for the speaker to finish and followed her out. She was not pleased to see me which should have finalized my decision for art school.

Undaunted, I went to Nyack and realized my ADD had me at an emotional 15 years of age. I needed to grow up, but when I did it was too late.

I had only one date with M. at a makeshift Simon and Garfunkel concert performed by the students. Afterward she went back to her dorm leaving me alone in the middle of the road.

Was I now resolved to find someone else? No, this fool thought God had put her there for me. My commitment to the Lord was not finalized, but His hand was on my shoulder. He should have given me a good slap in the face and said "What's wrong with you?" That slap came later when M. married N.

I went two and a half years at Nyack making a couple of good friends. One that comes to mind was Dwight Murray, a shy black man who befriended me in my Sophomore year. We were friends for many years though physical distance tended to keep us apart. I had the honor of him being the best man at my wedding. His death recently hit me hard since physical distance still played a part in our friendship.

Soon after my Sophomore year and after the first semester of my Junior year, I became a wandering nomad sometimes living in the streets, homeless. I was working for Nyack College with their Maintenance Department. The week before Christmas I injured my arm by slipping in the snow. I was unemployed for the next couple of months. During that time, the landlord of the apartment house I was staying out told everyone he was getting married and wanted the house back.

I had some compensation from unemployment, but nothing that would give me enough to find another room so I lived out of a backpack and an army blanket for a tent. I could only eat every third day and melted snow for water. Going home to my parents was not an option and there was no contact from them anyway though they were only 20 miles away.

At times, I would go to the men's dorm and acted like I had a room there sleeping in the end TV room. When I was called out on the third floor, I went to the second floor until I was sent out into the streets again. There was no Christian concern about my situation. I was told it was my own fault.

I had some friends from my days as an actor at the

college and was allowed to sleep on a moldy mattress at the Drama Props building, but I was seen coming out one morning and a "concerned" student ratted me out.

I was able at times to stay in the Music Building that was out of the way of the main campus. Soon, I was able to go back to work in the spring with a renewed pay check.

Eventually, I found an 8' by 8' room for $30.00 a month. The landlady watched religious programs every night with the volume up loud. At night, I carefully went to the bathroom and turned on the lights only to see a hundred cockroaches or more scattering to the far corners and up the walls. When it was warm enough I went back to the streets.

A year later, I found a night job moving medical products by forklift and sterilizing bottles for hospitals. When they asked me if I could drive a forklift, I said sure, how hard can it be? I didn't even drive a car yet. I took buses to the midnight to eight shifts. I learned to drive the forklift within the first shift.

The company closed after I joined them one year later. I helped the ladies from the assembly line with various games that they sent in for a lottery. Most of them never won but appreciated my help. One of them died at their station on the assembly line.

Eventually, I ended up living in Albany, New York. The worst soon would come and I allowed whatever happened as due punishment for my sins. I have never blamed the Lord for anything that has happened in my life. I read the book of Job and knew it could be worse.

I had a job at Fonda Del Sol as day manager for just room and no board. I thought I would get a paying job, but none were found in Ravena, N.Y. It was a small town and jobs were not there.

I was supposed to bring in entertainment and parties for those who lived in the various apartments. I decided that parties every Saturday night was best for everyone. I would over order food and drink so that I could take the leftovers back to my room. Much of it kept me fed until the next party.

I tired of the position and befriended a couple of teachers who said there was an opening at Voorheesville High School. I applied, got the job and moved to Albany. I was befriended by the Vice Principle, Don Belcer. He wanted me to teach seventh grade, but I did not have a teaching certificate. I filled in for various positions in the school and enjoyed the students.

However, I disciplined one student who threw a firecracker at a fellow student nearly burning his eye. That student was expelled and kicked off the baseball team. He lost his scholarship which brought his lawyer father to the school.

"Do you realize what you did to my son?" his father pointed his finger at me while Mr. Belcer stood behind him. I said: "Your son almost put another student's eye out with a firecracker. You know it's against the law." His father said: "He didn't know it was against the law." I said "Ignorance of the law is no excuse." Mr. Belcer's eyes widened in surprise. The father stormed out.

"Do you know who he was?" Mr. Belcer could not contain himself. "I don't care." I answered.

"He's head of the of the city council! The most powerful man in the county!" Mr. Belcer seemed impressed and not angry

"Then he should know better." I smiled.

Soon after, as I was walking home, I was shot at. The bullet pinged off the road and ricocheted into the library window across the street. I was able to hide behind a tree when the second shot buried a bullet into the bark. I saw a seventh grader that I kept after school for disciplinary problems aiming again in my direction from his home upstairs window. The police came and hauled him away.

    In the spring of 1977, I was walking down the hall of the school when I was told by another student that the brother of the student I had arrested was looking for me and he was carrying a gun. I had enough and went to Mr. Belcer's office and resigned. He was disappointed.

Chapter Five

There's A Kind of Hush

My own personal demons, like my brother, Paul, hide under the bed, inside the closet and creep around the attic at night. They are held at bay by my Lord and Savior, Jesus the Christ. I am methodical and diligent in my faith, yet I have failed to have continuous Bible time with the Lord.

I do not believe in Cheshire Cat smiles, loony speaking in incomprehensible tongues or hugging indiscriminate strangers. Part of that comes from old wounds and emotional scars from those I trusted and the cowardice they showed in times of stress and need.

> "Tongues, then are a sign, not for believers, but for unbelievers;….So if the whole church comes together and everyone speaks in tongues and some who do not

understand or some unbelievers come in, will they not say that you are out of your mind?"

I Corinth. 22.23

I mention this since I was with a community church in Albany, New York in 1975-6 called oddly enough The Community, that specialized with speaking in tongues to confirm your faith in Christ. Many faked it so they could be a part of the church. One dear lady named Nancy Bandiera, almost had a breakdown because she could not speak in tongues.

I befriended this young lady and assured her that speaking in tongues was not a prerequisite to being a Christian. If the Lord did not lead me to speak in tongues, then I concluded I did not have the gift. I realized later that I had the gift of discernment which made me uneasy at times.

My encounter with Nancy led to an opportunity in New York City in which she performed my one woman play Women of the Bible on off off Broadway. Unfortunately, not knowing the tickets were at the box office, I missed the performance.

Now back to my personal observations from having backs turned from me as life went on. These things keep me beyond humble to a stumbling paranoia. It brings on a spiritual loneliness bordering on snobbishness. My brother Paul was not spiritual so death waited at his door.

Paul killed our mother and older brother over financial problems which I will write more in detail later. Upon the deaths of my mother, father and brother, there were held wakes where family members would pay respects. I did not have the financial means and because of my willingness to testify on Paul's behalf made it dangerous to go.

Many wanted him dead. My testimony might have made him a lesser monster than they believed to be true. New York State thought differently, but that will be discussed later, too.

I knew and lived in the same environment Paul lived in. As a child you rationalize, but as an adult you brood and grow angry. I did not think this would come to such an end. It was a "horror house" long before the newspapers called it so after the murders.

Christ was not in that house. He was not welcome, yet my parents insisted we go to church. However, going to church gave my family limited access to forgiveness, love and spiritual fastidiousness. It, also, gave them a day of peace and quiet. Who knows how far our family could have gone if we were normal? If my family found the Lord as a means to change, to be happy?

Glenn, my older brother, had a great intellect as we all did which was gleaned from his poetry I found while snooping in his room. Yet he was an alcoholic and manic depressive which kept him living in the basement all his life in the family home.

My sister is talented or she would not have succeeded in business. Paul was an electrical engineer and my youngest brother was also successful in business. However, we are all damaged goods with psychological scars that will never heal.

The luckiest one was my youngest brother since he did not have to go through the worst years, but still had to see the emotional destruction left behind. He decided to live away from it all though he did inherit a great deal.

Our family was neither Catholic nor Jew, so we lived in the nebulous world of a safe Presbyterianism. Through spiritual blinding by God, I enjoyed the involvement with the Choir and Youth Ministry. I never heard the murmurings until I decided to go to Nyack Missionary College and was refused financial help from the church. Pastor Theobald gave me a few dollars to help with the payment of books and ease his guilty mind.

I was told later that it was because my family was not accepted by church members and I was dating a Catholic girl. I should have realized when I was in Eleventh Grade when Pastor Theobald announced I wanted to go into the ministry. He said: "A member of our church has announced his wishes to go into the ministry. It was not someone I expected, but it is Cliff Henning." There were no "Amens" or any joyful response.

The one he thought would make the announcement was my friend, Roy. No one came up to me after the service to say they were pleased with this announcement. In their eyes I assumed I was a leper.

My decision was not based on a religious experience, but I saw a man who had a large manse, a summer home and an easy life.

I couldn't blame them since my father was an excommunicated Catholic, my mother and brother were alcoholics and then there was the family curse. Again.

another disappointment in life which I tossed away into the back of my mind.

I did have a couple of moments in the pulpit with incomprehensible messages as "The Four Door Banana" and "Visions On A Desert Island" Pastor Theobald told me later that the messages were over the congregation's head. Though what he meant was that no one understood what I said. They were both criticisms of mediocre faith where the softness and easily bruised egos only open their hearts to false doctrine and sin.

I had a copy of the first message and later had to say I hadn't a clue about what I was talking about within the realm of my obvious incomprehensible intellectualism.

Within a year, the talk of being guided through the Presbytery and then seminary was out of the question. A Trustee's son was given the scholarship to further a career in photography. After the first year we were treated to photographs of nude models.

I was given a chance to be an elder when I was 27. My first meeting was a discussion on whether we should allow homosexuals to be leaders of the church. I said biblically we could not allow it. The elder who sat next to me said "Not everyone believes everything in the Bible." Pastor Theobald said it was up to the congregation and then asked for a vote to present the question. I said: "I vote no and resign" It took all of ten minutes as tenure as an elder.

I was goofy like that since I had not a clue about the depth of disappointment of those around me. To this day, I wander any church as a passing shadow. Not meaning they don't care, just indifference toward whatever life they were living. I have no feelings either way since if I were more involved, I could not write or draw as much as I have.

An explanation I needed here since most of the churches, except two, had many doctors and lawyers. I was in no one's social sphere for I write books few will buy and therefore not a living legend. Even this autobiography may end up on some dusty shelf along with my other 30 books. Yet, the Lord pushes me onward and I trust His judgment.

One thing I learned in life was that I was not perfect since I expected friends to come and go as they did. I was never important enough to hold onto as a friend so I learned seclusion. People in my past pop up now and again before fading away as I expected them to. I am seldom disappointed in that way. In my heart. I am still 15 years old with large boils on my face and back; a hideous beast that is looked on with pity or disgust.

The weird thing is that I do not blame the Lord for all this, but it put me in a room to write various works that gave me a sense of worthy various accomplishments. Even today I have seclusion in retirement to write and publish what I want to write. I may never see literary success, but I will leave a legacy for my daughters.

Now that I said that, this is the other side of my life. I dated some beautiful women in High School. I went to two Simon and Garfunkel concerts and at the second one Linda, my date, had back stage passes. I met Simon and Garfunkel and found Garfunkel rather chatty and Simon quiet. I had gone to Peter, Paul and Mary concerts whenever they were nearby. I met Paul Stookey after two of the concerts finding we had some things in common. At college I hitched to Beacon, New York to hear Pete Seeger and was able to talk with him. One concert I wasn't able to get back stage was after Bread, a short-famous band, performed in New York.

Each of these concerts, I had no problem getting a date, but I still felt ugly and thought the girls were on a pity date. When I grew my beard in my junior year at college, I felt differently.

I look back now and the scourge of boils was a blessing since I never thought to use or abuse women because of my insecurity and the respect I had for them. I felt it was an honor to be in their presence and would do anything for them if I could.

Chapter Six

College or Pandora's Box

Before I went to college, my mother was drinking and she looked at me and again said "You are different from the rest. I don't know what to say to you." I wasn't sure if that was good or bad.

She had instituted the cycle of self-loathing for even if we succeeded in life it was not enough. The exhilaration was to be crushed and we needed to tell ourselves it was dust. It was always the dead of winter where the trees were barren, the snow suffocated the sound of life and the stream of water rushed under thick ice not allowing any one of us to drink from it. Are you depressed yet? Don't be because it helped build the armor for me later in life.

"If you don't like it here, leave!" My mother's words

still resound in my ears, but where does one go when every town, every house, every room, every closet holds the terror of your past? Yes, God has forgiven me, but I have not forgiven myself. I feel guilt and loss of my family as if I plunged the knife of derision and hate into their hearts. Their anger for me had to be my fault because they accused me of such pain. This is how I felt the first third of my life.

I spent three years at Nyack and was just as lost except for a few friends who felt the same way as I did. Many of the students represented suitable denominations of which Presbyterianism was not one. I learned that many Christians were just church-goers, not to be disturbed.

I ran out of money and patience with Nyack when in the winter of 1971-72 I was told I had to leave the house I was sharing with four other students. The landlord's son was getting married and needed the house. It was Christmas week.

As I mentioned before, I had just injured my shoulder at work and could not find another place I could afford. My parent's home was 20 minutes away, but that was unthinkable. I knew I would be ridiculed and unwelcome with that decision so I became homeless. I lived mostly on the streets out of a backpack and makeshift tent.

At no time did I blame God for my misfortune. I turned to the Lord and expected to be watched over. My conversion was not an emotional one, but intellectual acceptance. I have always believed in God and never doubted that Jesus was the Christ. The real fault was that I assumed it was true and lived my own life at the time.

My problem has always been in so many denominations with all its rules and listed regulations related to conversion. I have visited many denominations as some believed in full baptism to be complete, others a simple dash of Holy Water on the forehead. Another faith demanded the need of speaking in tongues or full body convulsions. One or two demanded that financial success proved your worthiness.

Since none of this was my lot in life, I, too, have had to renew my conviction and conversion to Christ. Finally, I stopped beating myself up spiritually when I read:

> "And surely I will be with you always, to the very end of the age."
>
> Matthew 28: 20

Another image comes to mind when I found myself rejected by my fellow students in 1971. I ran into my old roommate, Richie Nawyn, who noticed I wasn't well during my sojourn of homelessness. He offered his apartment downtown for a while since he was getting married and wouldn't be staying there himself until after the wedding.

That weekend I was very ill, but God sent two students whom Richie asked to look in on me. I had a high fever and alcohol rubs brought it down. I had no insurance so the hospital was not a possibility so these two angels nursed me back to health. The Lord brought Richie to me at a time of need or I might have been found dead in the snow. This is why I feel the Lord has always been with me.

I felt sorry for myself when the day came when I snapped out of my malaise. I was sitting outside the Student Union with a stray half starving dog. One of the female students came out and expressed concern for the dog. She knew of my predicament yet said: "How terrible! I'll get a sandwich for him!" I asked if I could have one, too. She sneered: "You don't expect us to feed you!" It was that moment that woke me up and I realized I will always be on my own.

Fast forward to 1977, where I resigned from Voorheesville High School, a second time I would have been faced to live in poverty and without the job at Voorheesville High School, I would have been living on the streets again. I swallowed my shame and called home.

As I talked with my mother I heard my father yell in the background "He's not coming home here! I don't want him!" My mother, to spite him said she would come and pick me up. I still did not have a car.

My family quickly made me regret the decision to come home so I went back to college. I was a part time house painter so I could get a car. Again, I had no experience as a house painter but how hard could it be? I had to first get my license going through a driving school. This ended up being another lesson learned when my mother refused to help me practice driving her car. Everyone else in the family was helped, but I had to pay for a driving school.

In 1977, I met my wife, Judy, went back to college and worked two jobs. I was able to get a job in the kitchen of Kings College making salads and one or two meals. How hard could it be? Then I secured a chef's job at S.U.N.Y. College at Purchase where I had my classes. They knew I made meals at King's College, but never asked if I was a chef. How hard could it be to feed a thousand students?

I worked 40 hours at King's College and 22 hours on the weekend at S.U.N.Y. as well as going to classes full time and dating Judy.

Whatever it took not to go home except to sleep was my priority. However, I had a Siberian Huskie that was my pet from Albany. Her name was Hera, but she seemed to be abused, too, at that house and so I had to give her away.

Judy wasn't acceptable to my family either because they didn't give their blessing. Somehow, they thought I needed their assurance to allow someone into our family. However, I never received a blessing from them in anything.

After getting married, my family turned their anger toward my wife in subtle ways. Fortunately, she didn't hear much of the comments until after we left New York. The anger was never justified except maybe because we were happy together. They saw the love that escaped them over the years.

I have two daughters who never met most of my family because there was no interest by them from rumors and innuendoes that came from other family members. I heard of various relatives dying off, but I was told months after they were gone. It helped me realize why the silence for so many years. The lies my mother and family told them would have been proven false if I went to any functions.

I spent most of my life away from my family, but I put the Cross, the burden of their suffering on myself. As a Christian why could I not change anything? I realized nothing was the answer. Each of us had our hidden terrors and nightmares that refused to go away.

Memories for me are only nightmares that refuse to leave my side. Ghosts of the past wait in the corners when my faith staggers because I wish that the Lord could have saved my family as well. Now that time has faded as family members die off, They are only phantoms.

I will always wonder why few members of my family thought not to contact me. I have to think my mother had something to do with that, filling everyone with horror stories about my attitude and disinterest in them.

I yearn for what can never be. I savor for what I have with my wife and children. Yet, the Lord my God loves me still. You ask me how I can be assured of His love? Because I am still living on borrowed time as I am retired now with a loving family and memorable unique experiences that my Lord has put me through.

Unlike Paul, my brother, I do not feel worthless, the invisible man, the shadow that passes down hallways where people look through you instead of at you. It happens, but I tend to smile to myself and think it is their loss, not mine.

It has been hard to realize how much the Lord has shown me even at my age. I have learned so much about human behavior. The worst was when my father died. I was sent no flowers or messages, no cards. Only that he died from my brother. Paul.

When my mother and brother were killed there were no flowers, cards or visitations. I might've died that week without any last words or prayers. It is not out of bitterness that I add this, but I knew the Lord still had not forsaken me though others had.

I have put much of my personal history to give insight to where Paul was coming from in his letters. It is not out of paranoia since there was more to convey that would only bring a certain sensationalizing of my past. It was a difficult family history that shaped all our lives. Paul could not cope with the extreme verbal abuse he was forced to bear as he had to come home, too. So happened the tragedy of Thanksgiving, 2004.

What a team we as a family would have made if we loved each other, had faith and could forgive. Instead we wandered a world not big enough to keep us away from each other. I gave up the fight to allow God to bring us together or let things continue as they were.

> "If we live, we live to the Lord. So, whether we live or die, we belong to the Lord. For this very reason, Christ died and returned to life so that he might be the Lord of both the dead and the living. You, then, why do you judge your brother? Or why do you look down on your brother? For we will all stand before God's judgment seat."
>
> Romans 12: 8-10

I have brought out a part of my life to help the reader understand what my brother had gone through which was far more than I would have taken. I left when I was eighteen with short times at home during the summer. I could not take the insults and harassment though I would not have gone so far as Paul. Paul let himself suffer from the gossip and ridicule that even now rings true to those who had surrounded him.

Paul was considered the problem and cruelly reminded of it every day. This does not mean he was justified in killing anyone, but it happened. How could I comfort him, telling him to break away when he was so imprisoned with fear and guilt?

This is about a house divided upon itself and could not stand. This is about a double murder in Harrison, New York that a judge said was the worst crime in Westchester County history. Yet, out of a family that cursed itself, the light of Christ shone through. This is about murder, but, also, the sad circumstances before and after the event.

And so begins the family updates and gossip I received in letters from Paul. At a family get together, everyone had to wear name badges so they would know who was who. I, myself, had not seen my cousins since childhood.

It started to be serious in 2001 which shows how long it took before the final weekend of death. Paranoia might be too strong a word, but we were brought up to be suspicious about everyone. The family's motives were usually self-centered and selfish. I can add my own experiences to help substantiate Paul's mental state.

I was taught from an early age to believe the negative things as well as being worthless which was reinforced by my school and later, behind the scenes, my church. My family was considered one of those on the wrong side of the tracks.

My older brother, Glenn, got into trouble in class and the school assumed every Henning coming through was a troublemaker. Some of this may be repetitious so bear with me.

It started in kindergarten with another boy wanting my toys and told the teacher I wouldn't play with him. I mentioned the spanking in 2nd grade, but in 7th grade I forgot a pencil or pen for class. The teacher grabbed me by the shirt and slammed me against the backboard. He then pushed me landing in the garbage pail near his desk where I tore the seat of my pants. He noticed this and ordered me to turn my back to the class and bend down. The class laughed and then he put me outside the room facing the wall.

I mentioned the few incidents of being bullied from 6th grade to 11th grade. I learned to disappear so no one would notice me. I learned to put up a security wall until other students had to ask if a certain insult bothered me. I would say "What insult?" For I had put up such a wall that lasted throughout the years that I was not aware I was being insulted. It was my personal protection.

I tried to play sports but received only the chance to compete in ninth grade in track and field and JV baseball. I had a black coach in JV baseball who believed I would come around which I did. He cheered when I had my first hit and put his arm around me in celebration. He was not sarcastic but was truly happy for me.

However, High School baseball was different. If you were a non-Catholic you did not play. It gave me an idea to annoy the varsity coach no end. I asked my friend, Elias, a Jewish student to join the team more to irritate the coach than actually play which we were sure we would not. The coach allowed us to shag flies and practice hitting away from the main team. We stuck it out the whole season knowing we were driving the coach crazy without us complaining once.

I had no experience with the black community which kept me from the prejudice of my family. I heard comments from my father and mother because they had problems in the military. In 9th grade, I befriended the only black student in the school. We sat together in study hall sometimes laughing and joking until a couple teachers complained we were getting too close.

I was told it was not healthy to be his friend. I did not understand, but he was told the same thing. We never spoke again. I did not understand prejudice except to those who treated me badly. I still don't.

Whatever the problem, I took the responsibility of blaming myself. Since I spent my whole childhood hearing that I was a worthless human being, it must have been true.

I never once believed there was a reason to blame God for any decision I made. I was always given a choice and sometimes suffered the consequences. Sometimes, even now I wonder if retiring was the right choice. Then I toss that idea away. I am doing what I wished I could have done years ago which is writing and artwork.

> "For God did not appoint us to suffer wrath, but to receive salvation through our Lord Jesus Christ. He died for us so that, whether we are awake or asleep, we may live together with Him."
>
> I Thess. 5: 9,10

Chapter Seven

Arts And Crafts

Not all the anger and disappointments were bad for it pushed me first into the world of art. I could dissolve into an empty space where I could fill up blank canvases with other worlds and visions.

Mr. Dawson, my art teacher saw something in my work to encourage me as I wrote in an earlier chapter. Now I'll fill in the sketchy parts with more detail. Mr. Dawson set up art shows to display those who were talented. I sold my four water colors of mystical flowers through those shows. He entered me in a publicity contest for a local company and they accepted my design.

My church had an arts and crafts show in 1967 where I

entered painted t-shirts with various images and logos. I used enamel paint which made them very scratchy and really unwearable. Men in suits came to it and bought all of them.

In 1967, I branched out with music joining the local chapter of Up With People singing one of the songs "What Color Is God's Skin?" as a soloist. We toured the county singing in some nice areas.

In college, my friend Roy and his brother, Jay, started a folk group called IFF and asked me to join. We sang twice in public, but my not having a car to meet them across the Hudson River for practice broke us up.

In 1969, Nyack Missionary College had talent shows which various students did their own thing for the campus. I was asked to put together a show and decided to use a theme of folk music. I picked out the songs like "Something's Happening Here" and "Sunday Morning" Mostly protest songs which I didn't think would be a problem.

I turned down offers from music students because they were into classical music and would not fit in the theme of the show. Everyone was surprised that the songs were accepted by the college staff since it was a big departure from other shows. One thing that had to be changed was the song "Sunday Morning" to Monday Morning because the singer did not go to church in the song.

I made Day Glow paintings of images with the use of a black light to accentuate the songs. All of the 2x4 foot images were taken by students afterwards for their rooms.

Because of that concert, the next year, a Simon and Garfunkel show was put together by students that came across very well. They told me if we didn't have my talent show the year before, their show might have been refused.

It, also, led to drama. Murder In The Cathedral by T.S. Eliot. I played two parts and it was a great success. We performed two nights in a row. I found myself completely immersed in the role. The newspaper article concerning the play spelled my name wrong. The next year was the Glass Menagerie, but I already left college by then.

However, the director of Murder in The Cathedral asked me in 1970 to play Williams in a movie called None Were Heroes. The movie was about the capture of Major Andre. I still have the news clipping with all of us pictured. Again, my name was spelled wrong. They had me as Cliff Herring instead of Henning.

It was the same year that I published my first book, Images of Dreams, a poetry book. I believed then my future was in the literary arts. Alas, it was not to be.

In 1972, I published in Scotland my second poetry book, Black Mass Silhouette. Yet, before it was distributed, the publisher died.

I had a chance to join an improv group in 1974, but moved to the Albany, New York area. I ended at Fonda Del Sol as an event coordinator where in 1976, I tried to develop a children's theater starting with A Charlie Brown's Christmas play that I wrote. It was cuter than professional.

In 1977, I began to write The Saga of Everstream which ended up a 25-year journey into the world of Trags and Arbushi. I left writing poetry for the most part which served its purpose having forty poems published in various magazines and books.

In 1978, after leaving Albany, Nancy Bandiera moved to New York City and asked if I would allow her to do my one woman show on women in the Bible. I gave her the script. She set up Off Off Broadway and said she would send me tickets, however none came. As I said before, she left them at the box office and I didn't know it. I missed my debut near Broadway.

In the early '80's, I was tested for Mensa and with an IQ of 144 was asked to join. My wife was tested at 143 and I jokingly use that one point difference sometimes when we have discussions I don't want to lose. I needed something to brag about and Judy didn't need to, so, I joined Mensa.

Three years later, I quit because a high IQ doesn't equate to social graces. When it was found out that I was one of two Christians in the group, I was challenged to come to a home meeting where seven high IQ unbelievers would challenge my beliefs. I should have accepted, but I sensed a trap.

I tried to write contemporary novels including mysteries and ghost stories. I had hundreds of rejections I kept in a box. The few acceptances were for poetry to fill space in various magazines. It was not enough for me.

In 1998, I lay face down on my living room floor and cried out to the Lord that if my need to write was a useless endeavor then take it away from me. If what I am writing is not what you want me to write then show me or take it away.

The Lord said: "It was about time you asked me." Ideas flooded my head and I had to beg the Lord to stop or I would have been overwhelmed. Over half the books I have published, 33 to date, were from that day and still a few I haven't finished.

I sometimes think that if I don't finish them right away, I will live longer. I am not famous for in my prayer that day, I did not ask for a best seller. I still have a historical novel, a love story and a book of satirical cartoons to finish. I always thought I would be in the theater or the arts, but instead I was delegated to Retail for 25 years.

I was always told to be careful what you pray for and I thought about an addendum to that prayer of that year. I just leave it to the Lord and continue to write.

I look at my writing and the ability to draw and act within my daughter who seems to struggle with the many talents she has. My younger daughter is talented but has placed her abilities in other areas. They seem to be happy and that is all I need to know.

I am satisfied that, as I listed in the beginning of this book, I have created and published most of my works. I do have regrets about where and what I would have become if I stayed in Westchester County working in theater and the arts. However, I am still blessed with a family and library of my own writing.

Chapter Eight

And Now the Major Event

Now I turn to my brother, Paul who has had as many ailments as I have had. In his letter of April 8th, 2002, two years before that terrible Thanksgiving weekend, Paul said he was having liver and kidney problems. He had moved back into our parent's house because of illness, being overweight and long unemployment. He was taking so many pills for various ailments making it too difficult to function.

This letter went on and on about his illnesses until he finally finished and started his "crazy file" of the Henning family.

Letter of April 8th, 2002

"I came downstairs about three weeks ago and caught

mom 'mopping the walls' in the kitchen. She was using a floor mop." He stated that he was supposed to paint the kitchen, but back aches and diverticulitis was making it difficult. He had bouts of fatigue as well.

My mother was a child of the depression so there were two refrigerators in the basement filled with food that mostly had to be thrown out every few months. She was combining tubs of margarine to save space in the upstairs refrigerator.

Paul asked her: "Do you think a sane person would do this?" She would answer "You're no fun- there's no sense talking to you." And she would walk away.

Many times, Paul warned my wife and I not to eat certain things when we came to visit which was only once a year. Egg salad would be left on the counter too long as well as butter. Milk would be sour and the various meats were out of date so we started to meet at local restaurants.

My mother had peculiarities which led to the unfortunate events of 2004. My father died in 1998 and despite their bickering, she was a lot saner then. I do not want the reader to think my mother was really insane. She was a lonely woman bereft of family and friends. I did not realize how much we were outsiders growing up.

We had few visitors coming to our house. No one just dropped in to say hello or inquired about the family. Some of the reasons I will never know, but it had to have a difficult effect on my mother.

This is not to blame my mother or excuse Paul for this tragic event but shows the world we lived in surrounding our family. It was not helpful that I left New York in 1989 because I worked for a construction company that was soon to cut many jobs with the coming collapse of the building industry which I saw happening. I figured as a carpenter with a specialty of molding and finished work, I would find a job in Georgia.

I thought, because Judy's family invited us down to Augusta, Georgia, it would be a needed change. I thought it was a gift from God. Three months later my old boss told me the jobs dried up in New York and that I would've been let go.

In Georgia, I was unemployed for a year, but my sister-in-law, Elizabeth, put up with us during that time till I got into retail. She allowed us to stay in her house for longer than we should have, but she saved our lives. Grateful is too weak a word for it. During this same time, I had to sell my coin collection I built up over the years to pay bills and such. It showed both me and Judy that those things were not as important as our family. Judy told me recently as I was writing this of the time when she was sick and needed medicine, I did not hesitate to sell my last coin in the collection I brought down to pay for it.

In New York, my only source of family information was from Paul. I quickly became indifferent to the world I left behind. Whatever the complaints, I did not have to deal with them. Whatever the gossip, it never touched us directly.

Now, Paul was sending me letters about my brother, Glenn's mental illness. He informed me that our dad told him that Glenn started to be hospitalized when he tried to drink himself to death in 1990. He started taking anti-depressants.

Our mother protected him as she always did even to the point of giving him 1/3 of the house when and if she died. She believed he could not survive on his own as he started to drink again.

In his letter, Paul thought "All this mental illness explains all the fighting and beatings when we were growing up in the 60's and 70's. Crazy seemed normal. I am sure you remember "the strap" that mom would beat us with. (I think mom enjoyed beating us). Most of the time she was in a half-crazed half-drunken state. All the time I was growing up I couldn't remember a day my mother didn't roam aimlessly around the house or drinking. "

As a child, I remembered my parents arguing until my mom jumped into her car screeching down the road to who knows where. After I left for college, she turned her rage against Paul. I thank the Lord I survived the madness but had to leave the area to do so.

There was self-destruction in my family and all of us suffered our own periods of hell. The only way we could have broken the circle of destruction was through Jesus Christ, but that was not to be.

Paul wrote to me that at times our dad would join in at beating him up. One day, Dad saw Paul without a shirt seeing the bruises on his back and asked: "Did I do that?" Paul said "Yes." Paul then told me that Dad never hit him again. However, it was not out of love or regret, but that Paul might call the police.

My father never beat me that I remember, but I saw

the rage in his eyes a few times. He told me once that in the army, he fought another soldier and couldn't stop. There was always that inner rage from his belief of his own failure. Failure in marriage, business and faith.

My father never went to church except once when I was doing a dramatic presentation that I wrote for a Sunday night service. I was both surprised and nervous to the extent I forgot to give out copies of the songs we were to sing. My parents saw me afterwards and expressed the omission was forgivable.

Paul explained to me his trail of health problems. Though our mother had her problems, Paul mentioned that he thought she was a compulsive-obsessive where she was always buying food and storing them in the basement "like a squirrel for a winter that never comes."

She was always counting money and checking food lists. She was afraid to be by herself after Dad died though she hated him. Paul thought that was the reason she wanted him and Glenn to live in the house.

She washed clothes three times a day though most of them were already washed. She brooded over the littlest things and complained about everything. She had a nagging perfectionism so that if even if an ashtray was out of place, she would fix it.

She saw dirt everywhere so cleaned and mopped every day. We all knew she was lonely and being in the house all day did not help. I remember her looking out the blinds on the door hoping to see someone she knew come to the door. I have to think that our seclusion came from my dad's excommunication from the Catholic Church.

In the letter of May 21st, 2002, Paul began his own paranoia about terrorists. He discussed how New York City was using a Fuji blimp to monitor NYC bridges and having check points on bridges and tunnels. It gave me pause to bring my family up to visit.

This was the beginning of Paul's new obsession since he hardly left the house either. He had little contact with anyone to work out these obsessions. If he had, maybe the world he lived in would not have been so small and dangerous. Even the closet in his room was always locked and never opened if someone else was in the room. Later revelations explained why it was locked.

Anger and resentment built up over the years even into adulthood. The petty upbringing from my mom instilled almost a paranoia amongst us kids. We never lost the thought that everyone was against us. We couldn't grow up supporting each other.

The first time it came to a head was around July 25, 1999 after Paul had had a stroke. As he tells it there was a lot of "chaos and backstabbing". A family member called and yelled at our mother calling her all kinds of names. Paul took the phone and called this member a "psycho". The family member screamed "I hope you die!" with vicious name calling.

Paul got so mad that he slapped the phone off the wall cutting his hand. Blood was on the walls and floor as our mom tried to help him. Glenn came from the basement thinking Paul was attacking our mom. Paul grabbed a kitchen knife to keep "the creep" away.

As with me, Paul missed the day our dad died. He needed a ride to the hospital though no one came to pick him up. I didn't know at all until days later so I believed it was on purpose. Paul believed the death of my father and the debts he left behind caused such an emotional upheaval, that it is why he went off the deep end.

I didn't make it to my father's funeral since I was late being told when it was. Whether I went to the funeral or not would have brought the same amount of ridicule. I was never told dad was getting worse or that he was on the verge of dying. It was my punishment for moving south away from the family.

When my father died, few people spoke to me about it. There was silence at work where others lost family members there were cards and a congregational embrace of sorrow. I remember my store manager, Eric, came to me and expressed his sympathy, but other than that I suffered alone.

When my mother and brother were killed, I received a couple of calls, but no visits from anyone to my home. When I was fighting for my life in the hospital a few years back only my wife, children and my brother-in-law visited me. No one from my church, no calls from work except to find out when I would be back. Even I wasn't told I could've died until I was past the worst of it.

It sounds like I resented these things, but it reaffirmed my belief that the Lord still had work for me to do. However, too, was the life I led expecting the least. I let the Lord deal with it as I still had this shield of concealing the worst of my pain.

Back to Paul. He told me in a phone call that my mother threw out everything that was my father's when he died. Instead of mourning his loss, she cursed him for leaving her in debt. The family, for good measure, trashed me for not coming to the funeral not knowing my mom told me too late to be able to go.

This reminded me of when I went to college whereby I safely put my old comics of Superman, Batman and other superheroes in the basement. I boxed my old baseball cards of Mickey Mantle, Roger Maris, Yogi Berra, etc. putting them safely in a far corner. My mom threw them all out according to my brother because I dared to live away from the family.

I, also, had a complete collection of Mercury dimes except the 1916D which mysteriously disappeared from the basement. I could only sigh and shake my head over it.

All this nonsense I forgave long ago and prayed for their salvation which didn't seem to ever come. My father believed God had forsaken him and made his past excommunication from the Catholic Church a life of suffering with a loveless marriage, ungrateful children and lack of money.

My mother said she was too old and set in her ways and damned God for her suffering. Glenn was an alcoholic and manic depressive. He felt that no God could love him, no woman could suffer him so he stayed in the basement with his demons and alcohol. He refused to live outside or leave the comfort of his private cell. He never left the womb of our mother and it showed.

    We were all dependent on a parent who verbally and physically abused us. We seemed to ask for more abuse which we substituted for love. We stayed within her grasp of guilt, manipulation and self-depreciation. The result was that we felt cursed and unworthy of love or affection.

    When I was older and things looked brighter, a phone call and a harsh word would bring back the darkness of our youth. We did not hate her. It was worse, we became indifferent. I heard the cry for help from Paul but did not understand the danger.

    In his letter preceding the weekend of death, I did see a man on the edge. I was just glad I was not there. We have all been on that ledge without stepping over until that day. Paul stepped over, but no one was there to catch him.

Chapter Nine
Mixed Breed

    Unfortunately, I never wrote down Paul's conversation over the phone of his dreams. The reason was that it was difficult to take them as seriously as he did. Too much doom and gloom when I was having my own problems looking for work and trying to settle in a church that accepted "damn Yankees". This was an unbiblical southern sport at the time to "find the Yankees in your pew and abuse them"

    We did settle in a local church that accepted Yankees and southerners who could religiously co-habit and tolerate each other. Many of the members did not grow up in the south. Many are educated and well off financially. It took me a few years to realize they had the same heartaches and troubles as anyone else but allowed the Lord to help work through it.

However, Paul would tell me of his dreams where he had premonitions of jet crashes such as the Delta disaster in 1993 and car bombings in London. He thought of calling the British Embassy in New York City, but thought they would think he was the terrorist.

Some of our conversations centered around family history. Paul, as I wrote at the beginning, came across with the information that led to the discovery that our great grandfather on my mother's side was Jewish. I could not verify this because many of the family records in Germany were destroyed by two world wars. Whether or not any of it was true just brought a smile to my face hoping it was true.

As a Christian, I was thrilled by this knowledge which doubled the pride in my faith. However, this knowledge was not happy for my older brother who had some neo-Nazi leanings from the literature I saw in his room one year. Glenn must have believed it because he left the group that same year. Glenn was in his twenties at the time and searching for answers.

Most of my life I judged people by the way they judged

me. I had a certain intolerance when it came to betrayal of friendship. I saw no reason to waste time repairing friendships that only could result in more betrayals. As a Christian, I had difficulty turning the other cheek because it would it always be slapped again.

It only reminded me of the abuse through the first half of my life and I had to protect myself. It was not essential to pursue friends, for if they were friends I would not have to be the only one pursuing. It only told me that they could live without me.

My faith has kept in check the self-destructive response that surrounded my family in so many ways. I never wanted to complicate the crumbling world around those who found it difficult to ensure a friendship.

That crumbling world was quickly closing in on my brother Paul. When my father was alive I encouraged him to sell the house so that he and mom could go their separate ways. Having Paul and Glenn still in the house complicated things with a sibling war of words.

Paul, also, had more medical problems to keep them from selling. On October 31, 2002, he wrote that a cat scan showed an accessory spleen which was crowding out other organs. His letter listed all kinds of tests done and found a new disease, Cirrhosis.

Paul kept an in-depth record of his medical problems which excused him from exercising and losing weight. This added to his anxiety and the building up of anger that would explode two years later.

While Paul was accumulating his medical records and allowing himself to add a long period of unemployment living with our parents, I was determined to find fame and fortune experiencing neither.

Though, as I said before, I had some limited success with poetry in book collections and magazines, I started my most ambitious work of The Saga of Everstream. The first book entitled Whirlwind Sage and the Arbushi Wars took me twenty-five years to complete. The second and third books Tiathan Eiula and the Seven Fortresses Volumes one and two, took only a couple of years since the fantasy world I created made it easier.

I sent the books out to various publishers who insisted I would have to guarantee thousands upon thousands of book sales for them to publish my work. I sent the books to agents who told me the market was flooded with fantasy novels.

I've written and published over 33 books so far concerning fantasy, poetry, plays, commentaries and children's books. With the plays of which there were only four, since I was not willing to confine myself to the stage, one was entitled Whose Woods These Are which received an honorable mention in a national contest. Another, as I wrote about earlier, was about Women In The Bible was performed off-off Broadway by Nancy Bandiera in 1977.

In 1983, I started working part time for American Cablesystems adding commercials to local programs. They asked me if I had experience and I thought "How hard can it be?" From that I became a cameraman for an up and coming sports announcer. We went to Madison Square Garden to interview a local sports program winner from our town. I learned to edit programs and then develop programs. I produced informational shows for cable as well as a Christmas singing of Handel's Messiah which the community brought their own music and sang along. It had thirty showings during Christmas and New Year's weeks.

Having been a member of the Hollweg's Choir, I set up

a performance for Cable sans myself since I had to be the cameraman as well. When I became a carpenter for a construction company, I had to give it up.

I worked for Media Basics and was asked if I could manage the telemarketing department. I thought "How hard could that be?" Within two years I had quadrupled sales for him, but he stopped the commission sales, offered me only $250 a week and it was time to go.

The highlight of those years in the '80's was my time with the Hollweg's Choir that toured Westchester County and sang in New York City. The choir, also, had made two albums and cassettes.

The odd thing about being involved with the Hollweg's Choir was that I never heard classical music classified as classical music. It wasn't until my sophomore year in college that there was an after dinner when the play Murder In The Cathedral ended. The college nurse who was in the play put on Beethoven's Ninth and I mentioned I had never heard it before. It was at that party I was hooked on classical music.

For the past few years, I have written letters to the editor for the Augusta Chronicle for various political and religious causes. Through it all I give acknowledgment to the

Lord for choosing the right path even though wealth and fame escaped me.

There is a torment in growing up in a dysfunctional family that attaches to your soul for a lifetime. No matter how much the Lord comforts you, stands by you, sometimes it is not enough in your own mind. Betrayal seems to consistently be reinforced over the years which opens old wounds and poisons the soul. In writing, this shows the blessings of Christ that comes out of misery.

Sometimes I cannot sleep at night, not because of nightmares or dreams, but the void of nightmares and dreams. The Lord is with me as I worry for my children's future and their freedom to worship the Lord as they grow older. At this time Christians throughout the world are being killed for their belief as the rest of the world seems silent. The worst is yet to come only to bring the best in Christ coming again.

The Lord has forgiven my sins but being deserted by family and friends makes me wonder why the rejection. I am no one's priority except for Christ and my immediate family. Without them I would have nothing for I live amongst wolves that do not bother to wear sheep's clothing.

I am in emotional and physical pain each day. Yet, the

Lord, my God, helps me through each hour or I could not hold up to the void that my side of the family has left behind. Years of silence have passed and, at times, I peeled away the scars hoping for reconciliation only to have them dashed again and again. Yet, I pray for them anyway.

Sadly, with the continued mess of life, my talents were rarely used. As I said before, I was an actor on stage and screen in college, singer with Up With People, the Hollweg's Choir and IFF, carpenter, painter, artist (four art shows), writer of 33 books and counting, and a successful businessman, Yet, I was not satisfied.

The question comes down to this: How is this God's blessing? The answer is a small miracle that I came to Christ. Why? My family history did not involve Christianity. My mother, brother and father were not Christians. Should I feel guilty for not being able to save them?

How do you respond to the fact that part of your family condemned themselves? The answer is that it was their decision to reject God for whatever reason. I am sure angels wept over them for their loss. One other was saved though in prison and that was my brother, Paul. Being separated from my sister and younger brother I cannot speak for them.

If we had a loving environment, I suppose my reaction to the murders would have been different. Again, if we had a loving environment there would have been no murders. I put this disjointed family in a box and willingly opened it once a year. I was Houdini in a lost magic act. I was the son who everyone hoped would go away. Now the box is nailed shut and buried. The struggle has been taken from me and I must forgive and forget.

Chapter Ten

Wills and Other Ramblings

Now we are at the point of death, ignorance and instability. We must include grudges that never were forgiven and never healed. Some grudges aimed at me lasted over forty years from most of my family, yet forgiveness was not an option. It tended to be easier to think you never existed.

How much harder was it for Paul to live in the midst of anger and resentment? In a letter from my Aunt Mary we all found out that Glenn not only got 1/3 of our mom's house, but, also, had a major share of Aunt Mary's will. Glenn played everyone trying to get whatever he could so as not to be left in the cold. However, he felt everyone else should fend for themselves.

Intrigue became so fascinating as my younger brother was executor of my mother's will after Glenn was killed. My younger brother, also, received much of Aunt Mary's stash as everyone else was an afterthought. I was surprised that I was even mentioned in either will. My only stipend was being mentioned in my aunt's will.

Sharing was never in the top ten of our vocabulary and I was aware that I was only tolerated by my aunt so expected nothing anyway, Because of my sister, bless her this time, she made sure I was in my mother's will.

The chaos in our family was self-inflicted. Family members see the problems and manipulated the insanity to their advantage. The Lord, our God, was a vacuum in the emotional cataclysm of our family. How could anyone survive when hope and love was secondary to the needed yearning of acceptance.

None of us felt accepted and we had no idea how to find out how a family should be if we never experienced the closeness. The church, Jesus Christ and God had been summarily rejected to solve our problems because He seemed so far away as we were growing up. The feeling seemed to be mutual since God did not intervene, we took care of ourselves.

This was the year of paranoia for Paul because he constantly worried what would happen to him and his position in the family. He did not know if he would be taken care of if everyone turned against him.

It was obvious that Paul was not in Glenn's will or any of us for that matter. Since I was already cut off from the family, I expected nothing at all. I believed the Lord would take care of me and my family.

As I said, the chaos in our family was self-inflicted. Family members saw the problems, but only responded emotionally to the insanity. Paul told me of "secret meetings" with different family members where the intrigue was always fascinating. Paul's paranoia grew.

I lost the paranoia after I moved south to escape the madness. I was officially the Black Sheep of the family unable to participate or play the game of Family Feud. The relief was overwhelming since my own family had my full attention.

Paul's letters kept coming with discussions concerning

my mom how she thought her mom was a "sweetie". Paul thought she was delusional and I had to agree knowing a few incidents growing up. My father said his mother-in-law was a troublemaker and he was glad she was dead.

My mom told me she hated her father and to the last he baited her with these last words: "You're going to get your wish. I'm going to be dead soon." That last bit of guilt was echoed with the last conversation I had with my mom before she was killed.

The last thing she said to me was that she resented me not letting my girls visit her that year. I had thoughts that it wasn't safe. She refused to speak with my wife or girls just before that fateful weekend. This reminded me of the family I knew as it always centered around themselves and no one else. Our family history has consistent evidence of madness and anger.

My conversion was not emotional, but a long understanding of what Christ would mean in my life. Why should I shortchange Him or myself if I was going to commit to Him? I was naturally skeptical and wary of being manipulated because of that natural talent of my family. Distrust was part of our family crest in the form of a road kill fox.

Do I think I have angels on my shoulders? You bet! However, back to Paul and family matters. He sent me a letter from Nov. 2002 telling me that "Everybody is on their best behavior when you're here for a visit." I didn't know until a conversation on the phone with Paul that my mom could not take my visits with my wife more than a few hours. According to Paul, my mom would rant and rave about our visit making snide remarks tearing my family apart.

I thought this was happening from the conversations I had with my mom because they were tense and accusing. I assumed it was because I was happy and she was not. I visited out of a weird respect or obligation realizing that love was not in her vocabulary, but something to be bought or sold which was the saddest realization of my life.

One of the last visits, while we were walking around Playland in Rye, New York, she asked me: "You don't want to be here, do you?" I responded: "Not really because I don't get to see anyone else." My mom remarked: "It's because no one likes you."

I found that odd since I had been away for so many

years. Then I remembered the hatchet job when other family members talked with my mom and siblings, it was always derogatory as if I didn't care.

I realized, too, that there was jealousy involved. One, I was happy, and my children were normal. Two, we were Christians and though not wanting to shut ourselves off from the family, we showed we cared. It was rejected, but it must have upset them.

If it weren't for Paul, I would have been blissfully unaware of the angst I seemed to cause my family. It always fascinated me how Paul got family and personal information after I told him my wife was doing family genealogy. I wasn't interested in family quarrels, finances or intrigue. However, I saved everything in case of a family civil war. I never thought I would be using his letters for reference work involving this family tragedy.

Living down south was a great buffer to keep me out of the mess to come. In one of his letters from 2003, came the first clue of a troubled mind. He wrote in a P.S. the very following: "To be honest, I would rather die on the battlefield than having slowly wasting away health problems. (Surrounded by crazy relatives tormenting me every day like Harpies)"

Paul had a few health problems, but the worst was sitting in a house day after day mulling what he could be doing and because of his weight problems.

Soon. I was getting copies of my father's and grandfather's death certificates for my wife who does genealogy. Paul mentioned how he tried to help our dad while he was dying, but he, himself, had a stroke and suffered from diverticulosis. Paul said he "was being mocked by family members who didn't believe" he was sick. Paul mentioned they "mocked dad, too."

Paul cautioned: "If, at some point you were dying, I suggest not saying anything to anybody here. The psychotics here would mock you, too with 'He brought this on himself & He's getting what he deserved.'"

I later agreed with Paul on this point. I wasn't informed of my father dying until three months before he passed away. I did go see him weeks before he died, but the drugs he was on only kept him talking about his garden. I wasn't sure he even knew me. My Aunt Mary acted indifferently with my visit. Like all members of the family I was a blurb in their lives and easily forgotten.

When leaving, I hugged him, but it was not returned. When he ended up in the hospital, I was not informed until it was too late. I wanted to remember him alive so I did not attend his funeral. I did send a letter to him about the Lord and how his life lesson helped me to love my children. I wanted him to know his life mattered to me. My mom said she buried him with the letter, but I doubt it.

And yet I was the center of derision for not coming to the funeral. I would have rather remembered my father living than dead. The family made sure my absence was a form of insult to them all. If I went I would have been slapped in the face for coming.

Missing the last days of my father's life was meant to be a form of punishment not only for me, but my father, too. During his last days, it was made clear that mom and Glenn didn't want to do anything for dad. They had already written him off and wanted to get rid of him as soon as possible. Paul agreed with this thought since he was there every day.

One thing comes to mind as my dad lay dying in the hospital with my mom sitting next to him and that she wasn't there out of love. He begged to die at home, but she said no way. She enjoyed the attention of nurses and doctors around her.

Who knows what cruel things she said to him when out of earshot of anyone around her. When she did come home, everything that was in my dad's room was thrown out. Even the painted picture of Jesus I gave him when I was a teenager was thrown away. It hung over his bed for many years. She cursed him when she found out how much in debt she now was and how he played the lottery hoping to win himself out of it.

He told me on my last visit that he hoped to win enough to get everyone out of debt. It didn't happen. However, my mom asked me to send her a letter before she passed away. I knew better than to do this since she would pass the letter around to further mock and abuse me.

No amount of prayers seemed to change anything as the time was getting closer where death was at their door. Paul and our dad sat watching a Yankee game when my father turned and told Paul that "Your mother never loved me."

Interestingly enough on the death certificates of my

mother's father and mother were listed two different addresses. Our mom came from a dysfunctional family as well. I remember, too, that my grandfather had a girlfriend. I've seen her picture and knowing the domineering woman my grandmother was, I understand.

Paul wrote all this to me before going into prophesy and biblical dreams. Paul was looking for a new meaning in life finding later in prison to accept the Lord as the answer.

Chapter Eleven

More Reasons and Ramblings

April of 2003, Paul became more and more obsessed with what would happen if our mom died. He believed he and Glenn would "come to blows". Glenn was taking medicine for emotional issues and Paul noticed that the medicines were all out of date. Paul worried about having to defend himself if our mom died.

Quite a few evenings Paul said he thought Glenn was throwing pebbles at his windows. One time he threw a large pipe at Paul's air conditioner. Paul's answer was to pick up the pipe and any rocks that Glenn could use. "I, also, told mom if he didn't stop I was going to throw rocks at his car. Glenn started to park his car a block away."

His letter talked about a concern that "Mom has been buying rat poison to try and kill squirrels in the attic, but I told her with Glenn around here, maybe that's not a good idea."

Paul wondered why our mom continued to lie and feel sorry for Glenn. One morning, Glenn had a phone call and she went down to the basement to tell him. "Glenn woke up and went crazy—ranting, screaming and chasing mom out of the basement." Paul continued: "I know mom is afraid of Glenn but won't admit it."

Paul told me of the strange things happening in the house such as the time their washer died and Paul found our mom washing Glenn's dress shirts in the sink. Paul said "Glenn's going to love this." My mom answered "And you better not tell him!"

I inserted this bit of information because of the strangeness of a secluded family where friends and family members rarely came to the house. Paul was surrounded by events that were normal for us but would seem odd to anyone else.

Growing up, too, our family suffered through attempted suicides, multiple long-term illnesses, delusional psychosis and points of madness. What God seemed to offer our family was nothing but dissension, anger, hate, false love and deception. This was the atmosphere we lived in and Paul, through his letters, confirmed it never stopped.

Even our school treated us as inferiors. The only exceptions as I offered before were Pastor Theobald and the Castelli family of the Presbyterian Church. They treated me with respect and friendship which I have never forgotten.

God blinded me from the whispers about my family and its troubles. So then God could reinforce His love and care as I look back over the years. For what reason should I, even now, believe God is with me especially after the events surrounding the deaths of my mother and brother?

One reason is my wife, Judy, who amazes me with her love despite all that has happened and the two wonderful daughters He has blessed us with. My family is no reflection of the one I had to leave behind almost thirty years ago to come to South Carolina. If the Lord turned His back on me, He would not have blessed me with the family I have now.

We now come closer to the tragic events of that Thanksgiving weekend of 2004. One year before, Paul's letters spoke of his visions and dreams. July, 2003, Paul wrote about "looking off to the south was the Empire State Building" He saw a nuclear explosion envelope the whole area. Before it reached him, he woke up.

I found that the allusion of an atomic bomb a reference to the future of our family. It was a year before 9/11. Paul had similar dreams of disasters and I passed them off as his tension living in that house.

He was the only one who first told me that my Aunt Mary was dying. Since I wasn't informed sooner, my aunt thought I didn't care. It seemed imperative that I was kept in the dark about everything. No one cared to ask if all these rumors about me were true because my absence seemed to verify them all. I would have told them that I was quite happy trying to live a Christian life and the storm that was coming the next year was off my radar.

Paul's letters kept coming and with it more family history. I mention this episode because it adds to the dysfunction that seemed to follow us.

There was an accident on Aug. 30th, 1928 that our mom talked about for whatever reason. There was a car accident that killed Lillian Strong-Hughes (our grandfather's sister). It seemed everyone blamed her husband Frank. After the accident, which is now a family trait, Frank was an outcast and my grandfather Harry Strong said: "If Frank Hughes ever came around him again, he would kill him!"

Paul wrote to me how our mother kept falling down to the point he suggested bringing "spare tires from the basement and have mom wear them in an effort to keep her upright. If she does fall, she can bounce back up again."

Over and over he spoke about his failing health to the point of obsession. He wrote of his fear of losing the only place he could afford to live which was home. Yet, in a letter from Feb, 2004 he told me of flies in the house that he had to kill. They kept coming into the house to the point he thought he was "living in an Amityville Horror house." He thought he heard someone upstairs while washing his clothes in the basement. He knew no one was home, but he heard footsteps. When he went upstairs, no one was there.

Earlier in the year, Glenn blamed Paul for a dead battery and nails in his tires. Creeping paranoia was beginning to accelerate concerning Glenn and his racist attitude toward people of color and Jews. I was told my father was livid that a black man was my best man at my wedding. I wondered if anyone knew we had a Jewish heritage which was another target within the family.

Paul felt he was living with the mentally ill and that "mom should be in a nursing home and Glenn back at Grasslands." I was concerned about Paul, yet never realized he was the one who would snap a few months later.

Paul spoke of Mexican gang problems and drug dealing while people were being shot at Galleria Mall in White Plains. Our mother's Kleptomania was a popular subject which I knew from the three years I came back from Albany was true. Money would disappear or letters taken when I came back from Albany which I just allowed to make up for the rent I should have been paying.

His letters made me happy that I moved away because of the constant intrigue and family squabbles made it almost like a spy novel. Yet, I still didn't see the danger that was to come.

In Feb, 2004 letter, Paul told me of a relative's wedding to come, but I was not to know. Actual invitations were sent in June and I did not receive one. Amazing that moving away enhanced the anger and hate my relatives seemed to have for my family. None of this affected my girls and I put it to early family dementia.

I wasn't aware of family events because they feared I might show up. I probably would have taken the chance and gone up alone. It would have been free food and drink, maybe a chance to dance with Judy if we were both invited.

Paul's dreams were becoming more vivid that they included me in a plane that crashed into the Red Sea. Paul seemed to pull me in his nightmares and decided I should know about them.

Paul spoke of continuing harassment of Glenn until one night after pebbles were thrown at his window, Paul turned on the outside lights and Glenn ran away.

In a letter of March, 2004, Paul wrote of our mother trying to visit some relatives, but they wouldn't answer the door. Paul wrote that they must have been "hiding under a table with a crucifix, waiting for her to go away."

You, the reader, may think this is cruel to write about, but it is to show the instability of those who surrounded me and then Paul. The Lord shielded me from much of what Paul wrote to me about.

Again and again Paul wrote of Glenn's prowling around the house at night. Innocent or not, Paul thought he was a growing threat. Some nights Glenn came home and screamed at our mom because she waited up for him.

Glenn had such a paranoia that he told Paul that "I have everything booby-trapped in the basement in case anybody touches my stuff." Glenn, also, poured glue in his door lock and taped over it so only his key could let someone in.

The continual harassment between Glenn and Paul, who seemed trapped in my parent's house, whether real or imagined, put a mental strain on Paul. The letters as I read them again showed a progression to that Thanksgiving weekend of murder.

Paul's letters show the prison both Glenn and Paul made for themselves. I could only answer his letters with sympathy but could not offer him much help. Many of his letters tell about Glenn's obsessive cutting hedges and branches almost every day. "I began to wonder if anything was left. At times, around 5 AM, Glenn is raking the lawn."

In a June 1, 2004 letter, Paul starts his own obsession of terrorism which led to his stockpiling of various weapons in his closet. He writes of liberal bias in the news as well as problems in the Middle East. There became a drift from family news to terrorist plots with the possibility of an attack on America.

I was concerned about the triad of Glenn, my mom and Paul. There was so much tension and anger, yet I thought the threat might come from Glenn, not Paul.

In July, 2004, I received an odd phone call from my mom blaming me that Judy and the girls did not come to see her. We were having car trouble and I was in South Carolina working. Judy and the girls were in Cape Cod. Paul wrote to me in a letter that she thought I didn't want to see her and was going to cut off my allowance which was odd since I received no funds from her for anything.

My mom must have thought I was still a teenager since I never got a cent even then. I was suffering at this time with fatigue and bleeding from the colon. My ailments rivaled his, but I didn't want it to be a contest of who was going to die first.

In a letter of June 29th, 2004. Paul sent a letter that was mostly about North Korea and Nostradamus. At times, it was China and Russia destroying New York City. I didn't know what to say and I was fearful going up to visit.

On July 31, 2004, Paul spoke of the madness in the house which was, as I reread his letters, affected him, too.

My name was used often in an angry way which answered my question about my literary history and my family's reaction. I first published Images of Dreams in 1970, a poetry book with a rush of silence from my family. It was thirty years later that I published The Saga of Everstream with the title Whirlwind Sage and The Arbushi Wars. A second and third volume entitled Tiathan Eiula and the War of the Seven Fortresses Vol. 1 &2, were published in 2004, but the silence was deafening.

    I forgot the first rule of my family that no matter what the success in life, it doesn't matter. One must suffer the family curse of despair and worthlessness where no amount of success would be tolerated.

Chapter Twelve

The Madness Unleashed

    The tragedy of Thanksgiving, 2004, really started in July. Glenn and our mom decided to look into a reverse mortgage thereby cutting everyone out except them. Paul wrote about his fear of being kicked out of the house. Mom and Glenn needed cash so this would have been the easiest way to get it. It turned out they were unable to get it done.

    Paul wrote how Glenn still threw rocks and mud at his window to try and force him out. Our mom continually locked herself out of the house while Glenn looked up Paul's window as he sharpened the hedge clippers with a honing stone.

    Paul wrote that our mom and Glenn were arguing a lot. that mom threatened to call the police if he didn't stop throwing rocks at my window. Glenn told her to "Go ahead! Call the Police!" They had been fighting off and on since our father died.

Now this all sounds childish, but the Lord was nowhere to be found. The only world that existed for them was in the confines of that house. Arguments leading to a threat from our mom to sell the house and keep all the money was common banter. To say I felt blessed not to be there was a strong understatement.

Incidents of kicking doors because of being locked out, badmouthing of relatives, cursing me though I had not been around them for years kept coming up in Paul's letters. Even a family reunion could not be normal since everyone wore name badges. It was well known no one kept in contact with each other.

All this because the Lord was not sought after, but His name was used often in many conversations and not as a blessing. This is the wonder of how Christ came into my life. Would I have had an obsession like Paul in cover-ups, lies and deceit concerning the family and the world? His conversations about a terrorist plot against Harrison was ludicrous, but I ignored it though it was real to him.

From Nov. 5th to Thanksgiving, Paul told me of his concern of being thrown out of the house. It was so common, I almost stopped listening.

The amazing thing about our family is that we all tested with high IQ's. I was a member of Mensa for a couple years until I went to a large meeting where most of the members had the same emotional problems as my family. So much for being intellectually smart, but emotionally dumb.

Being intelligent couldn't solve our problems of wanting acceptance. We expected to be rejected in any endeavor we embarked upon. With me, my prayers comforted me with answers from my Lord. Most times it was not what I wanted, but it ended up worthwhile in the end as the Lord knew best.

Now we have reached the weekend of Thanksgiving. Paul and I talked once before and his obsession of the reverse mortgage was still on his mind. Then my mother called and berated me about last summer because I would not let my wife and kids visit. I did it because I believed they might be in danger.

She refused to talk with Judy or the girls which with

her last breath left guilt behind. It was her best talent. I only felt sadness and indifference. Sadness because for those who had endured the past forty years and indifference from me because I was neither the cause nor the focus by removing myself from the war zone.

We're all human whether Christian or not and we are capable of doing the worst of things. When fellow Christians steal from you, how hard is it to pray for them, forgive them? How hard is it turn the other cheek? How hard is it to listen to someone who steals and cheats others, sleeps with different women and uses the Lord's name in vain? Then listen to how they go to church and thank God in the same breath?

At least they go to church you say? Is it not the same as crucifying Christ again when your actions belie your faith? However, what was to happen was far worse. Now the horror began:

My sister called me the Wednesday after Paul was arrested. It was two days later which showed the struggle the family had in telling me at all. I was almost emotionless as she talked about what happened. It was if she were telling me about our neighbors instead of our family. We talked for a long time, but it was more informational than shock.

On Nov. 28th, 2004, Paul sent me a letter with an account from the police about what had happened. It showed me how clear his mind was when he wrote it.

Police account:

> Detailed to #87 Halstead Avenue to check on the welfare of Mrs. Grace Henning and Mr. Glenn Henning. Upon arrival I spoke to Mrs. Mary Tucker, the person who contacted headquarters and requested the welfare check. Mrs. Tucker stated she had not heard from her sister-in-law, Mrs. Grace Henning or her nephew Mr. Glenn Henning for three days and upon attempting to make contact at Mrs. Grace Henning's and Mr. Glenn Henning's residence she was turned away by her other nephew Mr. Paul Henning. Mrs. Tucker was concerned because in the past both Grace Henning and Glenn Henning had arguments which became violent. I asked Mrs. Tucker which door she had approached and she advised me the kitchen door. I knocked on the door and a white male (later to be identified as Mr. Paul Henning) came to the door and advised me that the door was broken and he would

speak with me through the rear kitchen window, I advised Paul Henning that I was there to check on the welfare of Grace Henning and Glenn Henning. Paul Henning stated that they were not home and he would not get involved in this. Paul then proceeded to throw out the window at me a prescription bottle full of pills and a pamphlet containing antidepressant articles. I asked Paul if the medication belonged to him and he stated "No, it's my brother's".

Here I'll condense some of the content where the officer called for his supervisor who came with another officer to search the house. While searching, one of the officers saw the outline of a gun Paul was carrying and asked if he had a permit. Paul didn't and was arrested.

The police searched Paul's room and found a rifle and a shotgun. In the past, when I visited Paul and went to his room to talk, I noticed the padlock on his closet door. He told me he kept his valuables in there and was concerned mom or Glenn were taking things.

The police gave Paul his Miranda rights at 2111 hours. From the police report: "While sitting in the booking room Paul advised me he needed to tell me something. At this time Paul stated: 'I killed my mother and my brother and both bodies are in the basement." The police searched and found the bodies while Paul was given his Miranda rights again at 2116 hours. Paul was videotaped and gave a written confession.

In a letter of explanation Paul sent me on Dec. 1st, 2004, Paul spoke how our Aunt Mary came to the back door demanding to be let in. My brother was holding a shotgun to the window and planned to shoot her as well.

The days during and after the trial there were newspapers that made my mother and brother out as innocent victims in the tragedy. Glenn was considered a quiet, mild-mannered and cordial according to the news media and those who worked with him.

We, the family, knew him as an alcoholic, manic depressive, violent and socially withdrawn. My mother was considered by her friends as well-liked, yet overly concerned about her children. We knew her as an overbearing, abusive, compulsive liar, manipulative and unloving.

I knew little of my brother, Glenn, except that he hid in the basement and drank. He was smart since I remember reading some of his poetry years ago. There's a torment in having a dysfunctional family that attaches to your soul for a lifetime. No matter how much the Lord comforts you, stands by you, loves you, but sometimes it is not enough.

Paul sent me a package while he was waiting for the police to either arrest him or he would try suicide by cop. Nothing was in the box telling me what he had done, but he did write "You better hold on to these." In the box were mostly his medical records.

I wrote and spoke with Paul's attorney sending him copies of Paul's letters to show his frame of mind. I did not think now or then that Paul should be set free.

Psychologists termed the killing of our mother a psychotic episode which is pure gobbledegook because the letters showed that it was building up for years. These psychologists formed opinions based on newspaper accounts where glowing reports were made of the victims while gossip and fairy tales from friends and family made Paul out to be a fiend.

I grew up in the same environment knowing the mental terror and physical abuse that we all suffered. There is no excuse for killing a mother and brother. I thank God I was not around to witness it. However, I wonder if my presence could have kept Paul from snapping.

The newspapers wrote that friends said that Paul had mental problems which was partially true as I reread some of his letters. What friends were these anyway? Were they hiding in the house and observed what was going on each day? Or was it the ramblings of family members that sparked this opinion?

The last two years before this tragedy, the brother I talked to was a bit paranoid, but that was a family trait. He talked of terrorism and family relations which kept me up to date. Paul did not sound psychotic, but desperate.

Few people visited our house growing up and with good reason, so where did all these opinions in the newspapers come from? The last time my mother talked with me was in anger and it was a week before she died. She left the memory of guilt and unforgiving sadness behind. It was her specialty.

Chapter Twelve

The Coming Storm

    In a letter of Oct.22, 2005, Paul wrote that his sentencing was quick and the judge declared in open court that this "case was the most horrible crime ever to come before him and maybe the worst in Westchester County history!" Paul declined to make a statement while leaving court under a "suicide watch".

    In the letter, Paul used Solomon's Psalm to finish his writing. Now this letter was a year later and surprised me that Paul looked to religion after a short time in prison. If he had turned to God sooner, this tragedy may not have happened. I wasn't sure if this was a new break with reality or a sincere cry for help.

    I incurred the wrath of the family by writing to Paul.

Soon I was sending care packages of food and money which, if they knew, would start off a firestorm. In time they found out anyway and decided to go apoplectic. I lost a brother, mother and father without the benefit of their salvation. I was determined not to let Paul join them no matter what the cost with my family.

Now the facts:

"Harrison Police Department Detective Report. Jan. 28th, 2005 Case 04-12198 DD#4611 Case description-Murder Class code-736

On 01/28/2005 at 1130 hours I spoke with ADA Robert Crisco in reference to this case. He advised me that I could release Grace Henning's vehicle and $600 located in Glenn Henning's wallet recovered by Medical Examiner.

At 1345 hours I met with Scott Henning...gave him the $600 and advised him he could remove his brother's vehicle."

So, Scott got $600 and the car. As the days progressed Scott and my sister Gail went through the house where I received a box of pictures, but nothing else.

I received letters in April of 2005 where Paul explained

the fateful day and some legal documents. During Paul's trial, a psychiatric order was made, but the D.A. objected because it would have benefited Paul. This information came from Paul when he was in the Westchester Jail. Paul wanted to explain that it was not spur of the moment, but a continuous stream of torment "that had no other outcome."

He explained he had "disagreements, but nothing like this. I had to do something to stop it. I'm being harassed by my brother, who's always attacking me. My mother was threatening to throw me out and give the inheritance to my brother by giving over the house or giving him the money from the reverse mortgage if she did that, stripping everything from me. I may as well be dead, too. I was keeping up the house, doing things to repair it. My brother was too retarded to do anything himself. He was a bellhop at Crowne Plaza."

Now I can't agree with all of this, but I was reading something that may have happened to me if I stayed in that lethal atmosphere. The Lord knew the possibilities that this madness could have incurred and took me out of it.

Paul worried about the reverse mortgage in which I thought was not as big a problem since I looked into it and my mother had a few roadblocks before it could happen.

However, I talked with Paul on the phone and he continued speaking of that day of death through the statement he made. This is a combination of his letter and our conversation to keep a continuous log of what he said happened:

> "Saturday (after Thanksgiving) I don't even remember. I think I stayed in my room all day because things were so tense in the house and I figured I'll stay out of it. Saturday, my brother worked. I would only come out for meals when my mother was out of the house shopping, at 10:00 AM while my brother was sleeping and then the second meal at dinner, after my brother left. About 4:00 PM I'd come out later.

> "Then Sunday, I figure my brother left and I'll do a wash in the afternoon about 2 PM. My mother comes down and starts trouble, arguing about the other day, in my face. She thought I had the original of the deed and reverse mortgages papers. She's getting madder and madder and she wants me out of the house.

> "I punched the side of her face. She went down screaming. 'I'll have you arrested!' I had never hit her

before. All this aggravation, hitting an 80-year-old woman, someone pushing you, always berating you, always berating me to relatives and her friends down the street at the senior group. I would hear this on the phone. She's threatening to call the police. I don't want to go to jail.

"I had a knife with me. I figured as long as my mother is there, my brother wouldn't come after me. If she's gone, he would. He's a maniac, agitated all the time. He hated my guts and wanted the house to himself. I don't think it was me directly. I kept a knife in a boot, if he came after me. I knew he carried a knife.

"I flew into a rage, pulled the knife and started stabbing her. She's yelling she wants to die. I wanted to die. I stabbed her a number of times while she's saying 'Now you're in trouble.' Mocking me. Why would she be saying this? I so mad at her, berating me all the time, even now. Okay, I wasn't working but I couldn't leave the house to work because they would lock me out with all that's going on. I would come home and all my stuff would be outside. I think she wasn't serious. It was really my brother. He and she would fight like mad. I couldn't understand it. I did so much for her. I felt betrayed by my mother. She kept saying: "Now you're in trouble.' I'm trying to stab her in the throat to shut her up."

I have no doubt about the strangeness of the events he describes. Our mother continuously tried to put guilt trips on all of us. Why not with her last breath? Even now, as a Christian, I see the rage Paul went through, but not justification in the crime. We had long talks on the phone of the troubles we all went through and knew there was no way to change how our family reacts to itself.

We were taught self-guilt, demeaning any success we might have and difficulty with our relationships. We could blame our mother so far, but most of us stayed close to feed on the strange, dysfunctional abuse to which we were addicted. Paul continued:

"Then when the blood stops, I figured she was dead. I sat there on the floor still talking to her as if she was still alive. 'How could you do this to me?' (He became tearful at this point).

"He then explained that 'I needed to clean the mess up because I'm like that. It sounds crazy. I dragged my mother onto a carpet and dragged her into the old bathroom into a shower stall (in the basement where Glenn lived) I sat in the chair awhile and started cleaning up again, putting some things in plastic bags. I sat for a while, thinking my brother would be home soon. I couldn't get all the blood up and there would be a battle when my brother comes home and he'll know something happened because of the mess and he'd come after me. I'm in fear of him. He's bigger than me and psychotic. I don't want to injure him, he'd overpower me. I should have left, but figured I had an attachment to my house. This is my home, too. I wanted to die there.

"I thought a long time, I'm not going to win this. I'm dead. But I didn't want to kill him, anyone else or myself, just not give him the satisfaction. So I was looking at my guns...I bought them in the 80's...just as fun guns. I would go to the range, but no self-defense issue. These guns wouldn't kill anyone. I was in the military, so I had experience with assault rifles. They were in the closet and I have a shotgun I would use for self-defense in the house and had it under the bed.

"So, I'm thinking about what gun to use. The assault rifle would go through walls and hurt someone else. So, I chose the 20 ga. shotgun. I waited for him to come through the second door. When he came in, as he walked through the door, I had the gun. I looked at him. He faced me, sneered at me and looked like he was coming toward me. I picked up the gun, got him right through the teeth."

When I was on the phone with Paul, the only time I talked with him while in prison, he told me, as if he was talking about someone else, that it was "a lucky shot". Reading this letter, it tells me he was lying. Guilt and smoothing the horror of it all was important to keep me from writing to him. How can God forgive this act? My answer was that He can forgive anything and it was important that I see this through. The Lord forgave me and watched over me all my life which leads one to believe there is a purpose in all things that we may never understand. Paul continued:

"He went down, blood pouring out. I was feeling sick to my stomach. It finally hit me that my life is over for sure. I could take an overdose and justify it in my head without it bothering me. But stabbing, hanging, I couldn't do that. I'm thinking about that, for and against. I'm still talking to them. I decided to stop my brother before he got me. If it was Scott or Cliff, I wouldn't have done it. Glenn was the town drunk. I'm not thinking of that. He was evil, like the bogey man, crazy things. I couldn't leave. That was my house, home. If they come after me, the police, I'll shoot it out and get them to shoot me. I couldn't leave there. It's my house. I'm running between floors with my guns, looking out the windows.

"The police handed it well. If they started shooting, I would be killed. The police came due to my aunt's call about a missing person Wednesday night,

He then described the subsequent events in which the police came to the house." According to the police report. Apparently, he was arrested on a "gun charge" for a pistol he had in his pocket at the time and, while at the police station, the following morning, he advised them about having killed his mother and brother. The police report continues:

"He, also, subsequently explained that while in the house, he thought he would 'maybe barricade the house. I started putting locks on the doors, nails and screws at the bottom of the doors and nail closet doors because the front door had a lot of glass in it. It would slow the police down so it would be hard for them and could shoot at the door to get them to shoot me. They don't shoot you unless you shoot first."

"He also stated: '...I wanted an end to it. I knew there was no solution to it. For three days I'm running between floors getting only catnaps, eating everything in sight, yet losing weight.' He spoke about his 'Aunt Mary' coming to the house during this time."

Paul further explained what happened when Aunt Mary came to the house asking where our mother was. Paul told me that he put his gun to the door and told her to go away. Aunt Mary later said she didn't realize how close she was to being shot. How much more tragic this could've been only opens up as Paul talks more about it. His letter continues from the report:

"He, also, explained that he killed his mother because 'I felt betrayed by the reverse mortgage gutting the Will...She's demanding I get out of the house. I blew up, felt betrayed, she's throwing me out without a car or job. I just slugged her... the ultimate insult. You strip everything from a person, then tell them they deserve it. They're not family, no longer my mother, just a thug on the street. I think the others detached from her, too, not coming to the house anymore...I felt the house was my home, like my brother and mother were intruders, not family anymore. I thought to leave, but it was my house, too."

He, also, consequently explained that "as a teenager Glenn would come up from behind me and hit me. He strangled me until I would lose all consciousness. He was 22 and I 16 or 15. He would kick me in the leg or sit at the table and stare at me when I was eating, to provoke me, but I wasn't provoked. I think all of this was to drive me out of the house so he would have the house. He already had one-third of the house. That's what drove Cliff away. I kept him up to what's going on with those letters."

There were a number of factors that drove me from New York. The main one was that I realized that my job as a carpenter was in jeopardy because the Northeast was on the verge of a recession. I just had a daughter who did not need to grow up in the vivid paranoia that was my family. It was evident that we were not welcome so it worked out for the best that we moved to Georgia.

I believed we were going to the Bible Belt and would find a safe haven. Unfortunately, the world is the same everywhere and I should have known better. His letter of information continued:

> "Throughout the evaluations, Mr. Henning related in good contact, with no evidence of disturbed thinking. He was somewhat depressed in mood and became tearful intermittently."

Paul sent me all this as well as the one conversation I had with him. I had no conclusion to make, just had to listen.

Chapter Thirteen

Statements

Police Report:

MEETING WITH MS. GAIL (Mr. Henning's Sister} MS. Box is 52 Y.O. recently married, previously married for 25 years. Her first husband died. She works as an "analyst and auditor for a relocation company."

She explained that she had seen Mr. Henning "Friday (November 26th) with my mother, Paul, my husband, Bill and her. We had breakfast. We had stayed at the house from Thursday night as we were at my cousins for Thanksgiving. Paul didn't come to Thanksgiving. Prior to that weekend, I saw him three months before." During that time, there was a change in Paul. We had tried to get our mother to sell the house and get something smaller, which I thought would make Paul and Glenn grow up. She was very concerned about Paul, especially in the last 5-6 months. He was moody, not coming downstairs. At the senior center, women kept telling me, when I went there, that I should get my mother to sell the house and get Paul out."

This part of the statement shows that Paul was not totally paranoid since our sister confirms that there was a concerted effort to move him out. Glenn had been there all his life, but my parents made no effort to move him out fueling Paul's paranoia even more. Now it still does not justify the events of that weekend.

In prison, Paul lost a lot of weight and stopped taking certain drugs for various ailments. Paul could have physically left the house if he lost weight and found a job. All this could have been avoided except the fact of the psychological intimidation that made family members who lived there feel insecure, worthless and mentally child-like with the inability to leave the premises.

It was a generational trend that probably started with our great grandfather on my mother's side. I saw it in our grandmother and grandfather who fought and berated each other and our mom. Our mom was a tormented woman who did not know love and never found it. She knew the power to control and destroy us emotionally.

We were sent to church, but that was only so she would have time alone. There were no great religious issues involved, just peace and quiet. If she did not need her quiet time, I might have moved in a different direction.

Gail's statement continues:

"I think it had an impact on my mother. She wasn't making excuses for Paul anymore, really now talking about selling the house. The past 1 ½ months before the incident, something changed between her and Paul, that she said she's tired of him and the situation. Also, she said that he wasn't talking to her and did nothing she asked, only coming down to eat. His relationship with them was always horrible as they never got along. After Friday's breakfast, during which everything seemed fine, we dropped Paul and my mother off. I went to the bathroom. Paul called me into his bedroom and he said: "Mom is trying to get a reverse mortgage and give Glenn all kinds of money." I said: "So what? It's her money. She'll give you something. She won't just throw you out." He looked scared."

This was, as far as I was concerned it was the final nail

in the coffin. Paul now believed he was cornered and confrontation was assured. The information continued:

> "It was different than he generally was about the house over the years and now maybe her selling it, especially since Dad died. He was different. He was worried, upset and seemed scared. Then I went downstairs to say goodbye.
>
> "Mom asked what I talked to Paul about. I told her about the reverse mortgage and her giving money to Glenn and she's getting like others, revengeful and nasty, and talking about the reverse mortgage and money to Glenn. I said "Treat us all equal, throw the guys out and use the money, don't play games with them.
>
> "I had no contact with them until Monday morning. The senior citizens were calling since they hadn't seen my mother. I asked, Monday night, my girlfriend, to go over. She saw the lights on and my mother's car there. Then Tuesday I asked the neighbor, who saw the car gone and then back again, but the lights on the first level and the kitchen were out. They are never out. Only Paul's light was on. I then called my Aunt Wednesday night to go over and call Glenn's job

Wednesday night. He hadn't come into work Wednesday. My aunt called, on her cell, saying that it was all dark in the house except Paul's room. She kept knocking and Paul started yelling at her from the window. She hung up."

The report continued: "I asked Ms. Box about her view of Mr. Henning and she stated: 'He always was alone and moody. He had been very sociable to others, but was now really cut off, won't talk or leave his room for a long time. He would agree to come to a family dinner and then, at the last minute, cancel. I think he's easily hurt or insulted and doesn't say anything. It's been crazy since our father died. Paul upstairs, Glenn downstairs. I thought of them needing help. They didn't want to work for years and I don't understand it. For years staying in his room, surviving on the hope our mother would leave him the house and some money."

In the report, it continues: "Ms. Box is a pleasant woman who related in a somewhat sad, perplexed manner, viewing her family as disturbed, but having little understanding of how to resolve the problems."

I found it difficult to understand that through the years

anyone in our family did not know how strange that these problems were. So many weird things have happened over the years, but if anyone was not in the family circle why would anyone believe it? If we had a loving and caring environment, I suppose my reaction to the murders would have been different.

The vision of that day is clear because I am very visual, able to picture what had happened. My indifference stems from lack of affection and actual separation that I had from my family all my life. Part of my soul shut down until I met my wife who filled most of it back up.

Still, there is a door in my soul I will not open. In it are all the nightmares and demons of the past that knock on that door in the middle of the night. It is then I gasp for air and doubt my salvation, fearing death because it is human nature to wonder why a loving God would accept such a bundle of imperfections. There are times I lack the devotion to God according to my standards, not His.

How could I condemn my brother when, in a way, I cut off my family for my own sanity? I put this disjointed family in a box and unwillingly opened it once a year to make an appearance. Since I felt I was no longer accepted as a son or brother.

I became the visiting relative who was treated politely while there and then scathingly criticized when gone. My wife was mocked and my children were made to partake of pitting one against the other with family politics. I can remember how my mother praised the beauty of one daughter and ignored the other. I refused to let her destroy the bond my girls shared.

I always wondered why the Lord could not get a foothold in our family. The answer was the reaction of the local Catholic Church and some of the things said in my own Presbyterian Church. One incident that answered my question was one Christmas Eve when I was 16 or 17 when Jim Knudsen asked me to be an usher at the Catholic Church.

I knew no better, so I went that night, picked up a long-handled basket and went down the aisle. I patiently waited as I put the basket in front of each family until they put something in. I ended up with the most collection than any other usher.

When the service ended, the priest sprayed the crowd with Holy Water until he came to me and somehow doused me with water. The priest later came to me and said he was impressed with what the other ushers said was a great amount in my collection basket.

The priest asked me my name. I said "Clifford Henning". He said with a quizzical look: "Are you Karl's kid?" I said: "Yes." He said: "You shouldn't be here." Then he asked: "What church do you attend?" I said: "Harrison Presbyterian Church." He contained his discomfort well and said: Please go and do not come back."

This incident I mulled over for years until I realized why my father wouldn't go to any church and why my mom would not go either. We were outcasts. Of course, my own difficulty with God should have answered my question. I needed reassurance constantly as if looking over my shoulder every day I would see Him there watching over me. I knew He never left me and at times carried me through the nightmare world I grew up in.

> "If you love those who love you, what credit is that to you? Even 'sinners' love those who love them...."
>
> Luke 6:32
>
> "Do not judge, and you will not be judged. Do not condemn, and you will

> not be condemned. Forgive, and you will be forgiven."
>
> Luke 6:37

However, having lived in that private hell I have been able to deflect insults and criticisms. A wall has been built where I pick and choose what I want to hear. At times, I don't even know I had been insulted unless someone else tells me that I had been. I sometimes remember screaming faces yelling "If you don't like it here, leave!" When I was 18, I took the offer.

Now Paul, not as an excuse for his actions, as an adult, suffered the same anxiety and insults for years as a captive in that house. Paul felt there was no way out because he was convinced that he was an insignificant loser. So, his anxiety ate away whatever was left until, as he told me, he weighed 300 pounds.

Paul became paranoid because his world became his upstairs bedroom where paranoia and the threat of terrorists preoccupied his mind. Hence the weapons and the need to protect himself carrying a knife or a gun on his person. The health problems developed to reinforce his belief of inadequacy and in the end, when threatened to be thrown into the streets, culminated into a last threat of prison by our mother was too much. His letters that I received showed his fears, but not the dangers.

To the end my mother laid guilt on me which was never resolved. To the end she forever slapped even more guilt on my brother as she was stabbed to death while encouraging the downward plunge of the knife. The words, the image never goes away since I am bonded with Paul in the tragedy of that day. We both wanted parental acceptance and were rejected. All that resounds in our heads are the insults and angry faces. They are there at night in the corners of my room and the dark cell of my brother.

I am not really indifferent with the total loss of my family which has been devastating. I steel myself by trying to wipe out the memory. The Lord has put this on me and I must continue. I cannot let my brother disappear within himself no matter what the cost.

Family members might read this book and say "I hope you both suffer." Again, forgiveness and filial bonds are not in our family's limited vocabulary. Instead, it has been greed, selfishness and control. If you cannot play the game successfully, you were dead in their eyes.

Chapter Fourteen

Psychology and Murder

Paul sent his psychiatric/legal formulation done by his lawyers. It is as follows:

"It is quite evident from the records and the interviews, that Paul Henning has been seriously emotionally disturbed for many years. He seems to have had some evidence of depression during his VA hospital clinic visits, as well as some neurologic problems with headaches, mild brain atrophy and numbness on his face, but the relevance of these findings is unclear to his mental state.

"It is clear that Mr. Henning, for many months prior to the incident, apparently deteriorated in his mental functioning, not leaving the house and, for much of the time, staying in his room. He apparently had had life-long problems with his brother, Glenn, who, also may well have had emotional purposes, but appears that it was not until Mr. Henning discovered his mother's intentions of acquiring a "reverse mortgage" and giving the proceeds to Glenn Henning, that Paul Henning became increasingly frightened and panicked that he would be "thrown out on the street." This was intolerable to him since he believed that he could not survive if he was put out of his home.

"The turmoil that he experienced, emotionally, was handled by him by social withdrawal into his room and avoidance of his mother and brother, until November 28, 2004 when, after accusations by his mother, he "exploded", killing her and then in a continuing panic, waiting for his brother to return home and killing him."

This observation acknowledges that my brother should have been put under psychiatric care instead of a state prison. Being in a prison would only add to his psychosis and it could lead to further dementia.

The letter I sent to Paul's lawyer could have given

proof that Paul should not go to state prison, but Paul pleaded guilty which his lawyer should have kept him from doing. Paul had written a comment on the back of these pages he sent asking for a food package and he mentioned what medications he was given:

> "I'm taking 'Prozac' and 'Trazodone' with downstate prisons. (Prozac doesn't work for me) At Westchester Correctional Facility I was taking 'Klanopin' every night. But downstate said 'They don't take inmates of such strong medicine.' I did get Trazodone which doesn't work well.
>
> The doctors diagnosed me with 2 things:
>
> A) Violent explosive disorder
> B) Suicide depression"

Paul wrote me another letter with his own description of the events of that last year. It appears that Paul needed to express his view of what happened. Something like purging. On Dec. 12, 2005 came the following information from him. I only add this to show the depth of his despair and how the Lord later held him in love.

"Part one of events of Thanksgiving deaths of

Glenn/Grace Henning. Nov.25, 2004 (Thurs.) Mom's goes up to a (relative's) home for dinner.

"Nov, 26th, 2004 (Friday) Mom and me go to IHOP for breakfast where mom hears me and our sister talking about the 'Will' and the fact that Glenn owns 1/3 of the house.

"Me and my sister go upstairs and I give her some copies of the will and ownership deed from Glenn. (I should of known better then to get her involved with her big mouth)

"As she leaves, she makes comment that she (mom) is getting like our aunt. I could see smoke coming from mom's ears. She was so mad at me.

"Mom later began to yell and scream at me that I was driving a wedge (within the family) and that she (mom) 'wished she was dead.'

"Nov. 27th, 2004 (Sat.) Stayed in my room most of the day to let mom calm down and avoid trouble.

"Nov. 28th, 2004 (Sun.) 4 P.M.: I needed to do wash and Glenn was at work (I don't go down into the basement when Glenn is at home because he starts trouble and I knew he carried a knife. (Glenn showed it to me)

"So, I would carry a knife in case he attacked me- It wasn't for mom! Anyway, Mom comes down to restart the argument from Friday. Mom begins to scream at me and 'orders me out of the house.'

"I felt this was the last straw of betrayal (maybe the stress and lack of sleep caused by Glenn and Mom made me snap). But, I did blow-up and punched Mom and she went down. Mom then threatened to call the police and have me arrested. (I knew hitting a senior would be a felony). I just went crazy. (Glenn and Mom finally pushed me off the deep end)

"I pulled my knife and began stabbing Mom while Mom continued to mock me with 'Now you're in trouble'. It was like she was daring me to continue to stab her and I was out of control as it was.

"After Mom was dead, I dropped the knife and sat down to think about what I did, I couldn't believe I did it and never thought I could kill her. (my mind was going a mile a minute and wasn't thinking straight)

"Nov, 28th, 2004-(Sun.): 4-11 PM: Later, I began to

think about what Glenn would do when he came home and decided to clean up moving Mom's body into the unused basement shower. At first, I was in a panic and began scooping up mom's blood with my bare hands and got towels and rags. I had blood all over me. I think I was in shock.

"I knew Glenn would come after me when he came home. It took hours to clean-up and I couldn't get all the blood out. So, out of fear I prepared for Glenn to come home. I got my 20 ga. shotgun and waited for him. I wanted to see what his reaction would be (I didn't know if he had a knife or even a gun).

"11 P.M.: Glenn comes into 'inner basement' door. I am standing to side of door-near basement stairs. (I cleared out some boxes to make room for me)

"When Glenn sees me, he 'sneers' at me in anger and then raises his hands as if to charge me. (Glenn did not see the 'pistol grip' shotgun in my right hand. I guess he thought he could attack me again.

"I quickly raised my gun and shot Glenn in the mouth and Glenn went straight down in a sitting position with blood flowing from his mouth. (at this point I was thinking suicide as a way out)

"I first put Glenn's body near the basement stairs and covered him with boxes while I cleaned up the blood.
"Nov. 29th, 2004 & Nov, 30th, 2004 (Monday and Tuesday) Cleaned up basement, also began moving mom's car to Food City Supermarket to make it look as if Mom and Glenn were maybe out. (I was stalling for time) I didn't know what to do and the bodies were too heavy for me to move far.

"I started to barricade the doors and to form a plan to get police to shoot and kill me. I, also, thought about turning on the gas and blowing up the house, but I didn't want to hurt people nearby. Over past three days, Glenn's body began to smell, so I decided to move Glenn to a nearby freezer because it had a lock on it. Glenn weighed about 240 lbs. and it took me hours to get him into the freezer, but I was desperate. (I know my reasoning sounds crazy, but I was buying time to think)"

Paul wrote this letter on back of the Harrison Police Department Detective report on 12/3/04. I found it incredible in the clarity of his writing where he was both murderer and observer of the events. Even as a Christian, how do you respond to something like this?

I would be criticized for writing to him in prison and the willingness to send some of Paul's letters to his lawyer. It was never my intention that he should be set free, but that he was in need of serious help which prison could not possibly give him. Perhaps I was in shock as well.

In his letters, Paul describes prison where he was living that maximum security was better because he had his own cell, better food and an older crowd of inmates. He said: "I find murderers to be the nicest and easiest to get along with." Since he was Class A felon he could not have a cell mate.

Paul explained to me about prison life and questioned why "my own family treated me so badly especially when I spent so much time in my room. Who could I have hurt so badly to bring out so much hate towards me (before the murders)?"

He said he was snubbing me, but worried how it affected my daughters. He said he hoped that they knew he was sorry and it was a "bad example of how to handle your problems in life."

Paul lost 100 lbs. in prison in which if he did it when he

was at home, he might've been able to go back to work and leave.

It was called the "Horror House" after those brutal slayings of mother and son. People would look into the basement windows thinking they might see something, perhaps a ghost. The house no longer exists having been torn down for a new building in 2007.

The reality of the years inside 87 Halstead Avenue were ones of heartache and sorrow. So, our house had collapsed, my father died of cancer, my mother and brother were killed, Paul is in prison, my sister and younger brother hide in silence and I was exiled to South Carolina. Yes, a house divided against itself….

Hardly an opportunity for Jesus to work and succeed in saving at least two lives despite the tragedy. One officially in 1977 though it was a lifetime blessing and the other in 2007 in prison. We almost survived the maelstrom and wait for the light of Heaven. Only the Lord is watching over us and no one else.

When my father died, everyone was silent with one or two mentioning condolences. When my mother and brother were killed, my Sunday School offered support, but I did not know how to respond. I expected a pastoral visit that never came. I expected too much since how can you comfort someone whose family members kill each other?

Later, as I wrote before, I was in the hospital with a serious illness that might have taken my life, but only my wife and daughters with a visit from my brother-in-law stopped by. Again, I expected too much.

I cannot blame my church since my job kept me from most church events and services. Perhaps, I appeared inaccessible. I have felt I was no one except to the Lord because of the chasm life put in front of me. Sometimes I wonder if the Lord was protecting me or those around me.

Chapter Fifteen

Aftermath

It wasn't until Nov. 2005 when I started writing to Paul. He was upset that I wasn't writing to him, but I had no idea at the time what to say. Was I supposed to offer forgiveness for what he did? Should I berate him for the crime? How does one react to a crime involving family members? I actually talked to him on the phone once, but he insisted on explaining exactly what happened that day. It was a chilling experience since Paul related the murders as if he was someone from the outside looking in.

As I mentioned earlier, it was emotionless and when he told me he killed Glenn with a "lucky shot" I could not hear anymore. He did not mean it was lucky at all, but that when he fired the gun it hit Glenn full in the face. Before that he told me when he stabbed our mother she looked him in the eye and said "Do it! Do it! Do it!" which knowing my mother is very much what she would say adding guilt and defiance to the very end. What she really said seemed to vary whenever he talked or wrote about it.

    I did not talk to him again. However, the last thing I heard was that his lawyer used me and my sister to take a plea deal. How, he didn't say. I mentioned this again because it was a horrendous life changing event that affected us all. There for the grace of God go I sort of thing.

     I learned a great deal about prisons and prison life through Paul. I couldn't send clothes, but food was okay. Paul noticed that inmates fed birds through their windows. Fights were everyday events which he tried to stay out of. Metal detectors were used before going into chow hall. He said the meals were varied, but some inedible. He hated Jell-O.

    If a deterrent could be used to keep even one person out of jail, Paul's letters should be the best illustration. The thought of living in an environment of inmate stabbings, riots and extreme violence between inmates should give anyone pause. In the Westchester County Jail, the jailers would routinely beat inmates, but turned off the cameras for the purpose of denial.

Paul was first on suicide watch, yet he helped other unstable inmates when the nurses asked for his help. Paul encountered murderers and rapists during 2005 and wrote about the facts of each case. During his time at the prison facility he became depressed and lost a lot of weight with low blood pressure. Paul lost 100 lbs. from 258 to 158 lbs.

It is strange that the reaction was mostly indifference. It felt like indifference though I could not really tell you how I felt. Since I had been battered verbally and emotionally for so many years, I had shut down all feelings to protect myself. I never cried over the deaths of any family member. I was not happy to hear about their deaths, but all I could give was a heavy sigh. I was surprised, since I had been unwelcomed for so long, that I was called at all.

Paul surprised me when he sent a letter with a section inspired by Proverbs. At the time, I was confused seeing this insight from his mind. His later letters showed he was surprised that I did not think he believed in God. My thought was how anyone who believed in God could do such a thing?

I could identify with him at a lesser level. In 1971, the worst time in my life living in a sleeping bag in the middle of winter, eating every other day and melting snow for water. I was not complete in my faith in Christ because of the rules and regulations of conversion according to the church. I equated conversion to bring success and happiness in life, but my first conversion brought homelessness and poverty for six years.

The difference with my brother is that he stayed in a place that would lead to death and prison. I cannot say what motivated his renewed interest in religion except that he could be forgiven in his crime and psychologically being released from his guilt.

My parents drove us all away until they were emotionally a dot in the distance and then we erased the dot. The joy of Christ is tempered with the tombstones of memories lying in the past. As a Christian, I savor my relationship with Christ, yet feel the burden of those friends and family members that rejected the change they saw in us.

There is the added guilt that something more could have been done. You read about the thousands of Middle

East Christians being killed for Christ and wonder if your faith will be tested as much. Then, with a sigh, you feel blessed that you live in a country where you are scoffed, at worst, for your belief and, at best, accepted by fellow brothers and sisters in Christ.

Jesus helps you accept the past you left behind though it never is totally wiped away. Never forgetting where you came from is an asset in your testimony as long as you know it has been forgiven in Christ.

The hardest part that my brother and I suffer with, tends to be forgiving ourselves rather than Christ forgiving us. This makes it harder to allow others to love us.

My void of affection and acceptance was filled up by Christ who brought my wife to fill the void that I didn't experience growing up. I am blessed with a longer life than doctors or my parents expected for me.

Each day I awake and say "Praise God. Thank you for one more day." I am not sad, but contemplative for what more can I do? I try to show my appreciation for what the Lord has given me. I just wish all of my side of the family could share in the relief of emotional pain and the knowledge there is another path to enjoy life.

We forget the beauty of a faith-based life. There is a major change as we look at the difficulties of Job and the thorn in Paul's side which shows life will not be perfect, but more than bearable. Perfection comes later when we rest with the Lord. We just have to look at each day as an opportunity to show appreciation by our daily encounters with those around us.

Paul writes to me that he is using the books I've written to reach out to fellow prisoners. Likewise, when I worked for Lowe's for almost 25 years, I gave out many books to customers and fellow workers. It took me nearly 22 years to realize that working in retail was a great mission field.

Frustration was the word for the first couple of years. I didn't realize that doing the right thing was contrary to the management's plan. Honesty was limited if you could sell a product for $300 more than the customer could afford. Bottom line was the most important thing.

However, when I started bringing in over one million dollars in sales, I was allowed to do what brought that success. I told customers that they did not need to buy

$2,000 in a washer and dryer. A $1,000 set would last just as long with fewer buttons to eventually fail.

Warranties were pressed as a means to a salesman's success. Even though I explained the good and bad for a warranty, I sold many. Lying for a sale was not necessary.

The real struggle with managers was their demand I spend less time talking with them. Unless I was talking about appliances, conversation was unnecessary as far as they were concerned. I was threatened with firing for not following their procedures many times, but they were fired for pushing employees to make sales no matter the cost.

The Lord had been with me for over the 24 years I worked. Unfortunately, He allowed some fellow workers to threaten and vex me. I realized that their lives were unhappy so I had to make adjustments. In the last year I worked, my life was threatened and reporting it made it worse. I had had enough and finally retired.

Now let's look at Paul who wrote to me on 2005 about where he was sent after the trial. First it was a medical center where he was on suicide watch for two months. Then he was transferred to an "IG" block which one of the worst in the local system. Amazing, to be considered a suicide risk to be put in where there were "fights and drugs and yelling all day."

During that time Paul became suicidal while holding back medicine to take "them all at once for an overdose." At the end of march 2005, Paul was sent back to the medical center. He lost his will to live during this time and weighed 100 lbs. less from refusing to eat.

I have read the doctor's report at that time and they expressed his bouts of depression "though denies suicidal intent." Paul was "preoccupied with his mother's will and the family conflict surrounding the family home." Paul felt "no one cares."

My writing to him seemed to lift his spirits. I told him he was not alone. I could not, even with what he did, abandon him like the family abandoned me. That November, 2005, had two confessions with priests and was educated about the Catholic religion.

I was surprised in Paul's conversion to Catholicism, but it later made sense since he could confess his sins on a regular basis to ease the guilt and suffering he was going through. It was logical he would go to the Catholic Church to ease his burden. What else would the Lord have me do? My mother and brother were viciously killed and I found out it was my younger brother! So, I prayed for my brother who still lived. I sent him food packages once in a while until now

I send one large package or two small food packages each month. He uses that to give a portion to the prison ministry for those inmates who are older and do not get packages or letters.

It is strange that my reaction to all of this was with seeming indifference. It felt like indifference though I could not really tell you how I felt. Since I had been verbally and physically abused for so many years, I had shut down all my feelings to protect myself. I never cried over the deaths of any family member who had become a stranger. I was not happy to hear about their deaths, but I was no longer welcome in their world. I accepted it because I learned to accept many things. I was of no use to them and so gave up that knowledge to the Lord.

I realized this was an incredible waste of family relations and now Paul was alone. Now what has all this self-aggrandizement meant over the first 160 pages of this book? I hope it has shown that despite misery, loss, success, failure and mist of loneliness for the first half of my life does not mean God is punishing but releasing a means to come to Him.

Yes, I am insecure at times because I cannot assess what I have done right or wrong. I know that accepting

Christ is primary in being saved, but also, the question of what have you done with that knowledge?

I spent 25 years with Lowes, a retail chain, and it took 23 years that I realized the Lord had me there for my mission field. I can't say I was a perfect missionary, but many people and co-workers have told me that my witness came through naturally. It's a good thing I didn't know what I was doing most of the time or I might have puffed up a little. I treated everyone the same, I complained when events of injustice occurred and I tried to give friendship and understanding to everyone. I had confrontations, but I had a strong sense of right from wrong. Of course, being human, I didn't always follow my own advice. Most times there were consequences when I thought I did things right.

I have some interesting memories in those 24 years with Lowes. The first year I worked for Lowes a black co-worker, Leroy, and I hit off right away. One day a customer didn't want his help because he was a N------. He then this yahoo came to me and told me he didn't Leroy to help him because he was a N...... I immediately told him I refused to help him either and to leave the store. He went to the store manager and as he spoke the store manager glared at me until the customer said the offending word. Afterwards, the store manager came to me and said "You don't have the authority to kick anyone out of this store." I said "I do have the right not to serve idiots."

This brings me to store managers in general. One other time I was going up on a cherry picker and happened to look across the way to see a different store manager making love to an employee in front of the office window on the second floor. I came down and told a female employee to go up and look to your right. She did and immediately came down and called the front office. Instigator, that's me.

My last year in the Aiken store, before I transferred to South Augusta, I was at odds with a store manager because he thought I spent too much time talking to customers. He objected to my "religious discussions" in front of employees and other customers. I, of course, refused to comply.

This store manager threatened to fire me if I did not stop. However, he like to play golf and made quite a few dollars during company time. One day the District Manager came in asking me where the store manager was, I replied, looking at my watch, "He might be on the tenth hole by now." He asked where and I told him. The District Manager told me later that he confronted him on the twelfth hole and fired him. I wasn't vying for sainthood, only justice.

During the years of complaints by various managers, who either quit or were fired, they came to me at different times to apologize for various insults and threats. My faith embarrassed them because I wouldn't back down. They said the reason they didn't fire me was because of the results I had in sales. I was fortunate enough to bring in $1.1 million to $1.3 million four years in a row.

The final reason I left Lowes before my 25th anniversary was a gentleman who seemed to think I wronged him in some way. He threatened my life twice with witnesses, but the management refused to do anything and that maybe if I quit would resolve the problem. I still don't know what prompted his anger, but I forgive him for it.

Customers still come to me since I retired and strike up conversations. Fellow employees still are happy to see me when I go to visit. I do have to say I miss some of them and certainly the intelligent conversations.

Chapter Sixteen

Last Words

I know why Judy was brought to me by God. She has been a steadying influence in all my decisions over the years. My decisions are based on her happiness and welfare which as such I have lived a more God-centered life than if I lived alone.

When I stand before God and He allows me in His presence, I hope to be given a small corner in the farthest realm of His Kingdom. I would weep with joy to have the privilege of being in that small corner.

I feel inadequate in God's view of things not knowing if I have acknowledged enough of what He has done in my life. My last words to those who read this is that I should never have been born except by God's grace and protection. I should not have lived this long except by God's love and intervention.

Even now, with all my illnesses, He has decided I should go on and this is my testament to His love and understanding of me. I seemed to walk through life knowing He was with me, but not voicing loudly enough His comfort, His blessings or His safety is what I think about. Hopefully, this testimony more than an autobiography will do what I should have done more of. So many things have been left out of trials, lost love and terrible events which would only sensationalize instead of witness two lives, Paul and myself, that have been touched by Christ.

At the time of this writing, my best friend from college and the best man at my wedding has died. My grief has not yet overwhelmed me. Neither of us saw the color barrier others saw. My regret we did not live close together so that we could support each other daily.

I now live in retirement, working in my walk-thru garden, spending much of my time with Judy and finding peace in the Lord in all things. At the time this will be published, I will have 34 books in print. Though reading books is a low priority for many, I will continue to leave a legacy behind.

Paul has settled in with a church group in prison and I hope it brings some peace in his life. As long as I can I will send him packages and money to make it easier for him in some way to survive the years in prison he must endure. How could any of us know the future whether we will suffer heartache or happiness. Suffice to know that the Lord is with us now and forever.

Made in the
USA
Columbia, SC